AGENDA FOR THE
THIRD MILLENNIUM

AGENDA FOR THE
THIRD MILLENNIUM

POPE JOHN PAUL II

Translated by Alan Neame

HarperCollins*Publishers*

HarperCollins*Publishers*
77–85 Fulham Palace Road, London W6 8JB

English translation first published in Great Britain
in 1996 by HarperCollins*Publishers*

3 5 7 9 10 8 6 4 2

The author asserts the moral right to be
identified as the author of this work

A catalogue record for this book is
available from the British Library

ISBN 0 00 627951 1

Printed and bound in Great Britain by
Caledonian International Book Manufacturing, Glasgow, G64

CONTENTS

INTRODUCTION
A Book for the Third Millennium

During the long pontificate of John Paul II there has been such a steady and abundant stream of up-to-the-moment teaching that many people, satisfied with what has been reported, quoted or commented on in the press, have felt no further need to read what the Magisterium has actually been saying.

This volume is offered to all who would like to know what the fundamental themes and basic arguments of the Pope's teaching are. It is by no means a fighting book. Rather, we present it in deep respect for the various religious views of its readers, and we are well aware of the many ways in which the work may be approached.

In it, the Catholic reader will find a book by the universal teacher of the Faith – that is, faith in the Lord Jesus and the Triune God. The Pope is the guarantor, with the bishops throughout the world, of the truth which is Jesus himself and which was taught by him and, at his command and 'inspiration', by the Apostolic Church.

Christians of other traditions will receive attention

from someone who recognizes ample opportunity for convergence and fellowship with them in essential aspects of the faith confessed in Jesus Christ.

Anyone who believes in God will be able to reflect on the teaching of a man who has contributed so immensely in the modern world towards making God's presence known as being at work in every individual's life and throughout human history.

Written by the Pope over many years of pontifical Magisterium and ecclesial ministry, the contents of the book are organized under ten headings.

The first heading is faith, as practised in the pluralist and tormented context of contemporary culture. Here the need arises to consider such topics as the relationship of faith to reason, of faith to the sciences, and of faith to today's social and cultural environment, so as to establish what truth is and to reaffirm love for the truth. Nor could this section in honesty omit an answer to the question, 'What is one to believe?' or reflections on the tragedy of ignorance.

The second section invites us to turn our thoughts to the Church with two aims in mind: first, on the basis of the Church as a divine gift, to make a seriously theological statement so as to overcome and put an end to the grosser forms of prejudice; secondly, to deal with such much-debated subjects as the laity, the ordained priesthood, theology and the theologian, women, catechesis, art, and the Church's troubles.

From faith and the Church we move on naturally to prayer in its whole range of possibilities, from the most imposing – its liturgical forms – to the most popular.

And with prayer, we turn to teaching on love; this ranges from God, defined as Love in St John the Apostle's first letter, to the facts of human sexuality, and the Christian ways of living love in religious consecration and in marriage, with the moral, pedagogic and religious types of commitment which are a consequence of these.

Further sections plunge us into the everyday world: the important values to which we must bear witness, the great topics and problems over which all the world's thinkers and statesmen meet and clash: history; evil; labour; the world and its complexities; and religions including their dangers, dialogue between different faiths, religious freedom and ecumenism.

Lastly, particular attention is devoted to the question of peace by reprinting the vigorous sermons which were to be preached by the Pope on his aborted journey to Sarajevo, and on the one that actually did take place in Zagreb.

This book is intended to be a gift for everyone. It will be for many people a challenge and a call to serve God. For others, it contains matter for discussion, dialogue and debate.

The Publisher

FAITH

To be able to say '*Credo*' – 'I believe' –
we must be ready to deny ourselves,
to give ourselves;
we must also be ready to make sacrifices,
to renounce ourselves and to have a generous heart.

Faced with the reality of atheism and pluralism in modern society and the difficulties involved in being really convinced and practising Catholic Christian believers, the magisterium of John Paul II teaches plainly, with tenacious and fervent constancy, the need to accept God's will, revealed in Christ and continually manifest in the doctrine and practice of the Catholic Church.

For Jesus has clearly said: 'Eternal life is this: to know you, the only true God, and Jesus Christ whom you have sent' (John 17:3); 'I have come into the world as light, to prevent anyone who believes in me from straying in the dark any more' (John 12:46); 'I am the way, the truth and the life. No one can come to the Father except through me' (John 14:6); 'God sent his Son into the world not to judge the world, but so that through him the world might be saved ...Whoever does the truth comes out into the light, so that what he is doing may plainly appear as done by God' (John 3:17, 21).

The difficulty of believing today

As we are well aware, contemporary civilization is permeated with different currents – not only Christian ones but also anti-Christian, non-Christian, non-religious and anti-religious ones. And sometimes these latter currents seem to dominate the thinking of contemporary society. This situation needs commitment if it is to be overcome: the commitment of all Christians who are aware of what it means to be a Christian. Christ says that his Father too has a 'culture', a culture in the deepest sense of the word: that culture which is the true perfection of the human spirit, its completeness in the natural, human sense and in the supernatural sense too.[1]

It isn't easy to be authentic Christians in the context of modern society, with the strands of renascent paganism running through it. But it wasn't easy yesterday either, when circumstances were different. It is harder still to create a wider social environment inspired by the great Gospel values. But we must strive to do this, putting our trust in the creative power that flows from the grace of the Risen Christ.

There are no types of society that can claim to be free of negative elements. Even roses have thorns.[2]

The tragedy of atheism

Today, in the world, and especially in our Western world, we realize the need 'to rebuild', in its essential components, a civilization truly worthy of human beings. Economic inequalities which still subsist and which will gradually get worse, are symptomatic of deeper needs impinging on the spiritual sphere. Materialistic ideologies on the one hand and moral permissiveness on the other have led many people to believe that it is possible to build a new and better society while excluding God and eliminating any reference to transcendental values. However, experience shows us all too clearly that, without God, society is dehumanized and the human person is deprived of his or her greatest riches. The closer human beings are to their Creator and Redeemer, the more truly human the future of the world will be.

Christianity does not deaden human nature but exalts its noblest potentialities, placing them at the service of the authentic progress of the individual and the community. 'In Christ, true man as well as true God, we can discover the full truth about ourselves and the purpose of our existence' (*Redemptor hominis* 11).

I urge you to preserve intact your faith in Jesus the Saviour, who died and rose again for us. Listen carefully to his Gospel, which the Church continues preaching to you with unchanging fidelity to what has been taught from the beginning. Bring up your children to obey the commandments, teaching them to ask God for the courage they will need to defy dominant opinion, when this is in opposition to the Gospel. Do not be afraid to swim against the tide.

Today as never before the world has need of the newness of the Gospel, so as not to drown in the overwhelming conformism of mass civilization.[3]

Some people claim to be seekers; others think of themselves as non-believers, or perhaps they are unable to believe or they are indifferent to religion. Others again reject a God whose face has been misrepresented to them. Others yet again, who are blinded by the outbursts of the 'philosophies of suspicion' which present religion as illusion or alienation, are sometimes tempted to construct a humanism without God.

I beg all of these people, in all fairness, at least to leave their windows open to God. Otherwise they are in danger of walking past the man in the street who is Christ, of cutting themselves off by attitudes of revolt and violence, and of being satisfied with sighs, impotence or resignation. Sooner or later, *a world without God is built against the human being.*[4]

Faith and reason

Between a reason which, in conformity with its own nature that comes to it from God, is directed to the truth and is accustomed to know what is true, and a faith which reinforces itself at the selfsame divine source of every truth, no basic conflict can arise. For rather, faith confirms the rights which are proper to natural reason. It presupposes them. For its acceptance presupposes that freedom which is proper only to a rational being. This said, it is nonetheless true that faith and science belong to two different orders of knowledge, which cannot be superimposed the one on the other. And here, furthermore, it becomes plain that reason cannot do everything of itself; it is finite. It has to be embodied in a multiplicity of partial types of knowledge and is expressed in a plurality of individual sciences. It can grasp the unity binding the world and truth to their origins only within partial modes of knowledge. In so far as they are sciences, even philosophy and theology are limited attempts that can only grasp the complex unity of truth in its diversity – that is, within a latticework of open and complementary kinds of knowledge.[5]

The 'learned' and the 'clever' have worked out their own view of God and the world, and they are disinclined to change it. They believe that they know all there is to know about God, that they have the final answer, that they have nothing more to learn. And this is why they reject 'the good news', for it strikes them as quite alien and conflicting with the main tenets of their *Weltanschauung*. The Gospel message proposes certain paradoxical reversals which their 'common sense' cannot accept.

As it was in the days of Jesus, so it is today, and yet today in perhaps a very particular way. We live in a culture which subjects everything to critical analysis, and which does this while often regarding partial criteria as absolute. By their very nature these criteria are unsuitable for perceiving the world of realities and values which eludes verification by the senses.

Christ didn't ask us to give up our reason. How indeed could he, since it was he who gave it to us? What he does ask is that we should not give in to the Tempter's old suggestion, as he flashes the deceptive prospect before us that we can be 'like God' (cf. Genesis 3:5).

Only those who accept their intellectual and moral limitations and recognize their need for salvation can make themselves once more open to faith, and in faith encounter, in Christ, their Redeemer.[6]

The Galileo case: science and faith

From the century of the Enlightenment down to our own day, the Galileo case has been a kind of myth in which the account of what happened has been very remote from the facts. Seen like this, the Galileo case was a symbol of the alleged rejection of scientific

progress by the Church, or of 'dogmatic' obscuran-
tism opposed to the free quest for truth. Culturally
speaking, this myth has played a considerable role; it
has helped to wed many a scientist, acting in good
faith, to the idea that the scientific spirit and its
research ethic are incompatible with the Christian
religion. *A tragic mutual incomprehension* has been
construed as reflecting a constitutive opposition
between science and faith. Clarifications afforded by
recent historical studies allow us to state that this
unhappy misunderstanding is now a thing of the past.

Galileo, who virtually invented the experimental
method, had understood, through his brilliant physi-
cist's intuition and by relying on various lines of reasoning, why only the sun could act as the centre of
the world as it was then known, or as we should say,
of the planetary system. The error of the theologians
of the day in upholding the centrality of the earth was
that of thinking that our knowledge of the structure
of the physical world is in some way imposed by the
literal sense of Holy Scripture. But we should remember the famous quip attributed to Baronius: '*Spiritui
Sancto mentem fuisse nos docere quomodo ad
coelum eatur, non quomodo coelum gradiatur.*' For
the fact is, Scripture is not concerned with the details
of the physical world, knowledge of which is entrusted to human experience and reasoning. There are two
fields of knowledge: that which has its source in Revelation, and that which reason can discover by its

own efforts. To this last belong the experimental sciences and philosophy. The distinction between the two fields of knowledge must not be understood as opposition. The two sectors are not at all alien to one another, but have points of contact. The methodologies proper to each allow different aspects of reality to be brought to light.[7]

I am happy to take as the starting point for my reflection one of the bronze inscriptions unveiled here today: 'Science and faith are both gifts of God.' This synthesizing statement not only precludes science and faith from regarding each other with mutual suspicion, but points out the deeper reason summoning them to establish a constructive and cordial relationship: God, the common foundation of both ... In God, therefore, despite their different paths, science and faith find their unifying principle.

If human life incurs enormous dangers today, this is not because of the truth discovered by scientific research; rather, it is due to the deadly application of technology. 'As in the time of spears and swords, so in the age of missiles,' the Holy Father said, quoting another inscription in the Centro Majorana: 'First to perish by these weapons is the human heart.'[8]

Rejecting the truth

The mystery of iniquity, the forsaking of God, has, according to the words in St Paul's letter, a well-defined inner structure and dynamic sequence: 'The wicked one will appear, who raises himself above every so-called God or object of worship to enthrone himself in God's sanctuary and flaunts the claim that he is God' (2 Thessalonians 2:3–4).

Here we find an inner structure of negation, of the uprooting of God from people's hearts and the forsaking of God by human society: and all this with the aim, as is commonly said, of a full 'humanization' of the human being – that is to say, of making the human person human in the full sense and, in a certain way, putting the human being in the place of God, thus 'deifying' humanity. This structure, of course, is very ancient; it has been known since the beginning of the world, from the first chapter of Genesis; I mean the temptation to confer the Creator's 'divinity' on human beings (made in God's image and likeness), to take God's place, with the 'divinization' of humanity against God or without God, as is clear from the atheistic statements of many of today's systems.

Those who reject the fundamental truth of things, who set themselves up as the yardstick of everything, and thus put themselves in God's place; who more or less consciously think they can do without God, the Creator of the world, or without Christ, the Redeemer of the human race; who instead of seeking God run back to idols, will always turn their backs on the one supreme and fundamental truth.[9]

The crisis in Catholic Christian faith

Even among many Catholics who still identify themselves as such, there is a remarkable weakening of faith in God as a person, and consequently of faith in Christ as the Son of God. They also find it hard to see the Church as a sacrament, an objective, not-to-be-manipulated gift from him. This is why, all too often, interior life or spirituality is equated with philanthropy and socio-political action in the cause of peace, justice, ecology and so forth, and why some people regard prayer, meditation and *lectio divina* as lacking particular importance.

Some lay people too, engaged in parochial, diocesan and national church structures, exhibit this secularized *forma mentis*, as also do some male and female religious who get more and more involved in social mission, which they often identify with their actual work as missionaries.

The publication of the new *Catechism of the Catholic Church* cannot fail to reassure and strengthen those of the faithful who have lost their bearings in the theological ferment of these latter years, and to bring back to the genuine sources of the faith those who have gone astray after false prophets.

In point of fact, studying theology, being a believer and feeling oneself to be an active member of the Church are three components which students sometimes find hard to integrate into their lives. We must not over-dramatize this: to go through a crisis can even be salutary and positive, inasmuch as it can make one's faith more mature and foster responsible Church membership. For this to happen, however, there must be careful pastoral support.[10]

The Faith: encounter with God in Jesus Christ in the Church

Opinions, private points of view and speculations no longer suffice for anyone weighing up their effect on the course of human life, and whose respect for humanity is awake. They certainly do not satisfy anyone who is conscious of being able to arrive by means of theological responses at the first cause of the truth. God has manifested his word to us. We cannot find it and grasp it unaided by the power of our intellect alone, however much may be conceded to our diligence in illuminating the credibility of this word and how it corresponds to our questions and to our various forms of human knowledge. It is in the inner logic of Revelation that the defence and interpretation of this word require the special gift of the Spirit. It follows, then, that the study of Catholic theology must always be subject to a willingness to listen to the binding testimony of the Church and to accept the decisions of those who, in their capacity as pastors of the Church, are responsible before God for protecting the deposit of faith.

Without the Church, the word of God would not have been handed down and preserved; one cannot want God's word without the Church.

Intellectual comprehension of the faith must of course be integrated with another aspect: the faith, besides being known, must be lived. In the New Testament itself a faith based uniquely on knowing would be rejected as a perversion. For example, according to the Letter of St James, the demonic forces know the One God but, since they do not accept this knowledge with their inner nature, all that remains for them is to tremble before this God. For them punishment, not salvation, is in store (cf. James 2:19).

When God addresses his word to us, he does not tell us some fact about things or other people; he does not communicate *something* – he communicates *himself*. Thus God's word demands a response, which ought to be given with our entire person. The reality of God eludes those who confine themselves to thinking of his word and of his truth only as objects of impartial research. On the contrary, the way to draw near to God as God is by worship alone. One of the great mystics, Meister Eckhart, used to urge his listeners 'to get rid of the imagined God'. If God remains purely and simply 'he', we remain alone and empty. God gives himself to us as 'you'. We only find him when we too say 'you'. It follows, as Eckhart used to say, that we ought to have God present 'in our heart, in our search and in our love'.[11]

Learn to know Christ and make yourselves known to him! He knows each one of you individually. This is no knowledge giving rise to opposition and rebellion, a knowledge from which one needs to flee in order to safeguard one's own personal mystery. This is no knowledge composed of hypotheses which reduce human beings to socio-utilitarian dimensions. His is a knowledge full of simple truth about human nature and, above all, full of love. Submit to being known by the Good Shepherd; his knowledge is simple and full of love. Be sure, he knows each of you better than you know yourselves. He knows because he has given his life for you (cf. John 15:13). Allow him to find you. At times people, young people, lose their bearings in the world surrounding them, in the vast network of human affairs enveloping them. Allow Christ to find you. Let him know all about you, let him guide you. True, in order to follow someone, you must at the same time make demands on yourself; such is the law of friendship. If we wish to travel together, we shall have to give thought to the road we are taking. If it leads up into the mountains, we shall have to follow the signposts. If we have to climb a mountain, we must not leave the rope behind. And besides, we must keep in contact with our divine friend whose name is Jesus Christ. We have to co-operate with him.[12]

Christian faith and courage in life

We have to make a conscious decision that we mean to be professing Christians, and we must have the courage to be different, if need be, from other members of our social group. Our decision to bear Christian witness presupposes that we perceive and understand the faith as a precious opportunity in life, transcending the views and manners of our environment. We must take every opportunity to experience how the Faith can enrich our existence, make us genuinely steadfast in the struggle for life, strengthen our hope against attacks of every kind of pessimism and despair, and prompt us to avoid all extremism and to commit ourselves thoughtfully to furthering justice and peace in the world; lastly, the Faith can console and cheer us in sorrow. And so it is our task and opportunity in this diaspora situation to experience more consciously how the Faith can help us to live more fully and more deeply.[13]

The first thing I want to offer you is an invitation to optimism, hope and trust. Certainly, the human race is going through a difficult patch, and we often have a painful impression that the forces of evil, in many manifestations of social life, have got the upper hand. All too often honesty, justice and respect for human dignity have to mark time or seem to be on their last legs. And yet, we are called to overcome the world by our faith (cf. John 5:4), since we belong to him who by his death and resurrection obtained for every one of us the victory over sin and death, and so has made us able to affirm humbly, serenely but certainly, that good will triumph over evil.

We belong to Christ, and it is he who conquers in us. We must believe this deeply; we must live this certainty. If we do not, through the problems which are constantly arising those insidious beasts called discouragement at, tolerance of, and supine adaptation to the arrogance of evil will worm their way into our souls.

The subtlest temptation afflicting Christians today, and especially young people, is precisely that of giving up hope in Christ's affirmation of victory. The author of all guile, the Evil One, has long been fiercely committed to dowsing the light of this hope in each individual heart. It is no easy path – that of the Christian soldier. But we must follow it, knowing that we possess an inner strength for transformation, communicated to us with the divine life that we have been given in Christ the Lord. By your witness, you will make others understand that the highest of human values are taken up in a Christianity lived consistently, and that the Gospel faith not only offers a new vision of humanity and the world, but more important still, makes it possible to bring this renewal about.[14]

Love of truth is love of Christ

There is also a pollution of ideas and manners that can lead to human destruction. The pollution is sin, which generates falsehood.

Truth and falsehood. We must realize that falsehood very often presents itself to us under the garb of truth. Our discernment has to be the sharper, therefore, so that we can recognize the truth, the word that comes from God, and shun the temptations that come from the Father of Lies. I have in mind that sin which consists in denying God, in rejecting the light. As it says in St John's Gospel, 'the true light' was in the world: the Word 'by whom the world was made but whom the world did not acknowledge' (John 1:9–10).

'The truth contained in the Father's Word.' Yes, that is what we ought to say when we recognize Jesus Christ as the Truth. 'What is truth?' Pilate asked him. Pilate's tragedy was that he had the Truth in front of him in the person of Jesus Christ and couldn't recognize it.

This tragedy must not be repeated in our own lives. Christ is the centre of the Christian faith, the faith which the Church proclaims today as she has always done, to every man and woman. God was made man. 'The Word became flesh and dwelt among us' (John 1:14). In Jesus Christ the eye of faith beholds the human being as it can be and as God wishes it to be. At the same time Jesus reveals the Father's love to us. But the Truth is Jesus Christ. Love the Truth! Live in the Truth! Carry the Truth to the world! Be witnesses to the Truth. Jesus is the Truth that saves; he is the whole Truth to which the Spirit of Truth will lead us (cf. John 16:13).

Dear young people, let us seek the truth about

Christ and about his Church! But we must be consistent: let us love the Truth, live in the Truth, proclaim the Truth! O Christ, show us the Truth. Be the only Truth for us![15]

The human being, 'a pilgrim of the Absolute'

Human life on earth is a pilgrimage. We are all aware of being in transit in this world. Our lives begin and end, they start at birth and go on till the moment of death. We are transitory beings. And on life's pilgrimage religion helps us to live in such a way as to reach our true destination. We are constantly kept aware of the transitory nature of this life, which we know to be extremely important as the preparation for life eternal. Our pilgrim faith directs us towards God and guides us in discharging those choices which will help us to win eternal life. So, every moment of our earthly pilgrimage is important – important as to its challenges, as to the choices we make.

In the Revelation of the Old and New Covenants, we who live in the visible world amid temporal things are also deeply aware of God's presence penetrating every aspect of our lives. This living God is in fact our last and absolute bulwark amid all the trials and sufferings of earthly existence. We yearn to possess this God once and for all, the moment we experience his presence. We strive to attain the vision of his face. In the words of the Psalmist: 'As the hart longs for flowing streams, so my soul longs for you, O God.'

While we strive to know God, to see his face and experience his presence, God turns to us to reveal his own life to us. The Second Vatican Council dwelt at length on the importance of God's activities in the world, explaining that 'with the divine revelation, God wished to manifest and communicate himself and his will's eternal decrees with regard to the salvation of mankind.'

This notwithstanding, this merciful and loving God who communicates himself through Revelation still remains an inscrutable mystery to us. And we, pilgrims of the Absolute, keep seeking the face of God throughout our lives. But, at the end of the pilgrimage of faith, we reach 'the Father's house', and being in this 'house' means seeing God 'face to face' (1 Corinthians 13:12).[16]

From the very beginning, the human race has been called by God 'to subdue the earth and master it' (Genesis 1:28). We have received this earth from the Lord *as a gift and as a responsibility*. Made in his image and likeness, we have a special dignity. We are master and lord of the good things placed by the Creator in what he has made. *We are collaborators with our Creator.*

This being so, we for our part must never forget that all the good things that fill the created world are *the Creator's gift*. For so Holy Scripture advises us: 'Beware of thinking to yourself, "My own strength and the might of my own hand have given me the power to act like this." Remember the Lord your God; he was the one who gave you the strength to acquire riches, so as to keep, as he does today, the covenant which he swore to your ancestors' (Deuteronomy 8:17–18).

How apposite this advice has been in the course of human history! How *especially* apposite it is at the present day, with our *progress in science and technology!* For as we contemplate our brilliant achievements, the works of our mind and of our hands, *we seem to grow more and more forgetful* of him who is the author of all these works and of all the good things which the earth and the created world contain.

The more we subdue the earth and master it, the more we seem to forget the Lord *who has given us the earth and all the good things it contains.*[17]

Jesus, the way that leads us to the Father

We 'reach' God through the truth about God and through the truth about everything outside God: about the creation, the macrocosm, and about human nature, the microcosm. We 'reach' God through the truth proclaimed by Christ, through the truth that Christ actually is. We reach God in Christ, who continually assures us: 'I am the truth.'

And this 'reaching' God through the truth which is Christ is the source of life. It is the source of eternal life, which begins here on earth in 'the darkness of faith', to reach its fullness in the vision of God 'face to face' – in the light of the glory where he abides for ever.

Christ gives us this life, for he is life, exactly as he says: 'I am the life.' 'I am the way, the truth and the life.'

Jesus is the Son of God and he is of the same substance as the Father. God from God and Light from Light, he became a human being to be the way which would lead us to the Father. During his earthly life he spoke ceaselessly about the Father. To him, to the Father, he directed the thoughts and hearts of all who listened to him. In a sense, he shared God's Fatherhood with them, and this appears particularly in the prayer he taught to his own disciples: the Our Father.

At the end of his messanic mission on earth, the day before his passion and death, Jesus said to the Apostles: 'In my Father's house there are many places to live in; otherwise I would have told you. I am going now to prepare a place for you' (John 14:2).

If the Gospel is a revelation of the truth that human life is a pilgrimage towards the Father's house, it is also a summons to the faith by which we journey as pilgrims: a call to pilgrim faith.

Christ says: 'I am the way, the truth and the life.'[18]

Christ's Cross – a message of sorrow and salvation

Although he was the light to enlighten all nations, Jesus was destined in his own day and in every age to be a sign disparaged, a sign opposed, a sign of contradiction. This had been true for the prophets of Israel before him. It was true for John the Baptist and would be true for the lives of his future followers.

He performed great signs and miracles: he healed the sick, multiplied the loaves and fishes, calmed tempests, restored the dead to life. Crowds flocked to him from everywhere and listened to him carefully because he spoke with authority. And yet he met harsh opposition from those who refused to open their hearts and minds to him. Finally we find the most tangible expression of this contradiction in his suffering and death on the Cross. Simeon's prophecy came true – true regarding the life of Jesus, and true regarding the lives of those who follow him, in every land and in every age. So the Cross becomes light; the Cross becomes salvation. Isn't this perhaps the Good News for the poor and for all who know the bitter taste of suffering?

The cross of poverty, the cross of hunger, the cross of every other sort of suffering can be transformed, since Christ's Cross has become a light in our world. It is a light of hope and salvation. It gives meaning to all human suffering. It brings with it the promise of an eternal life, free from sorrow, free from sin.

The Cross was followed by the Resurrection. Death was vanquished by life. And all who are united to the crucified and risen Lord can look forward to sharing in this selfsame victory.[19]

Faith in the Holy Spirit

The Church unceasingly professes her faith that there exists in our created world a Spirit who is an uncreated gift. He is the Spirit of the Father and of the Son; like the Father and Son, he is uncreated, without limit, eternal, omnipotent, God, Lord. This Spirit of God 'fills the universe', and all that is created recognizes in him the source of its own identity, finds in him its own transcendent expression, turns to him and awaits him, invokes him with its own being. Humankind turns to him as to the Paraclete, the Spirit of truth and of love; human beings live by truth and by love and without the source of truth and love cannot live. To him turns the Church, which is the heart of humanity, to implore for all and dispense to all these gifts of the love which through him 'have been poured into our hearts'. To him turns the Church, along the intricate paths of humankind's pilgrimage on earth; she implores, she unceasingly implores uprightness of human acts, as the Spirit's work; she implores the joy and consolation that only he, the true Counsellor, can bring by coming down into people's inmost hearts; the Church implores the grace of the virtues that merit heavenly glory, implores eternal salvation, in the full communication of the divine life, to which the Father has eternally 'predestined' human beings, created through love in the image and likeness of the Most Holy Trinity.

Yes, we groan, but in an expectation filled with

unflagging hope, because it is precisely this human being that God has drawn near to, God who is Spirit. God the Father, 'sending his own Son in the likeness of sinful flesh and for sin, condemned sin in the flesh.' At the culmination of the Paschal Mystery, the Son of God, made man and crucified for the sins of the world, appeared in the midst of his Apostles after the Resurrection, breathed on them and said: 'Receive the Holy Spirit.' This breath continues for ever, for 'the Spirit helps us in our weakness'.[20]

Ignorance, religion's worst enemy

Each of us needs an integral and integrating training – cultural, professional, doctrinal, spiritual and apostolic – equipping us to live in a consistent inner unity with ourselves and also, whenever necessary, to give reasons for our hope to anyone who asks us.

Our Christian identity requires us to make constant efforts to train ourselves more and more thoroughly, since ignorance is the worst enemy of our religion. How can one claim truly to love Christ if one is not committed to knowing him better?

Training and spiritual life! These two things are inseparable for anyone who aspires to lead a Christian life which is truly committed to forming and building a more just and more brotherly society. If you wish to be faithful in your daily lives to the demands of God and to the expectations of humanity and history, you must constantly nourish yourselves on the word of God and the sacraments, 'so that Christ's word may dwell in you abundantly' (Colossians 3:16).[21]

Religious commitment

Religion: this is not hot news, sensational today and forgotten tomorrow. The Faith is not some teaching to be adapted to one's needs, as occasion dictates. It was neither invented by us nor created by us. The Faith is the great divine gift which Jesus Christ has given to the Church. St Paul says in his Letter to the Romans: 'The faith comes from preaching, and the preaching in turn comes from the word of Christ' (Romans 10:17). Believers find their foundation in Jesus Christ, who lives on in his Church through the centuries till Judgement Day.

The Faith draws its life from the traditions of the Church. Only in her can we be sure of finding the truth of Jesus Christ. Only a living branch of that tree, the Church community, can draw strength from her roots.

Today I exhort you to hold fast to the Church's Faith. This is what your mothers and fathers did before you. Keep the Faith yourselves and hand it on in turn to your children. This is the reason for my pastoral journey to you here: 'I want to make clear to you, brothers, what the message of the Gospel that I preached to you and that you accepted is, in which you stand firm' (1 Corinthians 15:1).

Without a firm faith, you will have no standards, and you will be a prey to the varying teachings of the day. Admittedly, today there are indeed some environments where the true doctrine is no longer accepted, and where new teachers to suit every taste are always being run after; but these will beguile you, as St Paul foretold. Do not let yourselves be deceived. Pay no heed to the prophets of egotism who put a distorted interpretation on the development of the individual, who offer an earthly doctrine of salvation and who want to build a world without God.

To be able to say 'Credo' – 'I believe' – we must be ready to deny ourselves, to give ourselves; we must also be ready to make sacrifices, to renounce ourselves and to have a generous heart.

For those who are brave enough for this, the darkness dissolves. Those who believe have found the beacon assuring them of a safe journey. Those who believe know which way to go and can get their bearings. Those who believe have found the right way, and no folly of whatever false teacher can ever mislead them any more. Believers, having a sure foundation, are prepared to live their lives in a way which is worthy of a human being and pleasing to God. Aware that their lives are drawing to a close, believers can assent when God calls them to himself.

True, it must be admitted that life in the Church today is not the most comfortable way of living. It is less trouble to adapt to circumstance and take cover.

Nowadays accepting the Faith and living it means going against the stream. To opt for this needs strength and courage.[22]

II

THE CHURCH

Of this Church we are members and children;
by this Church we have been begotten
to supernatural life in Baptism
which has grafted us into Christ.
We should therefore love this Church
as our Mother.

In revealing the nature of God and the significance of human life, Jesus has proclaimed the Truth for all time and all peoples. And, to maintain intact and secure that Revealed Truth, which also includes the means of eternal salvation, he has founded the Church on Peter, the Apostles and their successors – that is, the Bishop of Rome, Successor of Peter, and the bishops who are in union with him. Therefore:

(1) The Church is sure and certain, since it is willed and founded by Jesus Christ, who did not write down any of his own words or command them to be written down, but who has promised the presence of the Holy Spirit, the Spirit of Truth, who will

maintain and develop the Truth Revealed within the Church, according to need and demand.

(2) The Church is indefectible – that is to say, it will endure until the end of human history, despite defections, hostility, protest and muddle. For there is the divine assurance: 'Go therefore, make disciples of all nations; baptise them in the name of the Father and of the Son and of the Holy Spirit, and teach them to observe all the commands I gave you. And see, I am with you always; yes, to the end of time' (Matthew 28:19–20).

(3) The Church is infallible in the sphere of Truths to be believed and of Morals to be practised. For, of all the Apostles to whom Jesus gives his threefold powers of Teaching, Ministering and Governing, he chooses Peter and to him alone gives the powers or 'charisms' which in their turn imply another three-fold immutable mission: Peter is the foundation-stone of the Church's unity, he is the universal Pastor with full responsibility for souls, he is assisted in an absolute way so that he cannot err in the field of Truth and can strengthen the whole Church. Plainly, the powers given to the Apostles have been passed on to their successors, the Bishops and priests; and the powers given to Peter have passed down to his Successors, the Bishops of the See of Rome.

The mystery of the Church

There are people who mistakenly suppose that Christ can be separated from the Church, that one can devote one's entire life to Christ without reference to the Church. In so doing, they forget the truth proclaimed by St Paul in the words: 'A man never hates his own body, but he feeds and looks after it; and this is the way Christ treats the Church, because we are parts of his Body' (Ephesians 5:29–30). As I stated in my recent Apostolic Letter on St Augustine: 'Since he is the only mediator and redeemer of mankind, Christ is the head of the Church; Christ and the Church are one sole mystic person, the total Christ' (*Augustinum Hipponensem* II, 3).

So, loving Christ means loving the Church. The Church exists for Christ, so as to continue his presence and witness in the world. Christ is the Spouse and Saviour of the Church. He is her Founder and her Head. The more we come to know and love the Church, the nearer we shall be to Christ.

The Church is truly a mystery, a reality both human and divine, deserving to be studied and contemplated, yet nonetheless going far beyond the grasp of the human mind. St Paul, for instance, speaks of the Church as 'a field' which is tilled and made fertile by God (cf. 1 Corinthians 3:9). He calls the faithful 'the temple' of God in which the Holy Spirit dwells (cf. Ephesians 5:21–23).

In point of fact, St Paul often identifies the Church

with Christ himself, by calling her the Body of Christ (cf. Romans 12:12ff.). He also calls her 'our mother' (cf. Galatians 4:26), since, thanks to Christ's love and the waters of Baptism, she gives life to many children in the course of history. By means of these and many other symbols, we come to see, in a limited yet real way, the great richness of the mystery of the Church.

The Church is essentially a mystery of fellowship.

The fellowship we share in the Church is both vertical and horizontal: fellowship with the Three Persons of the Most Holy Trinity, and fellowship with one another in the Body of Christ. To be in communion therefore implies a deep personal bond of knowledge and love.[1]

Loving the Church

The Church, handing on the message of Revelation with which she has been entrusted, is the place of God's living presence in the human world, and the place where redemption takes place. The Church, as the Second Vatican Council states, is 'in Christ, in the nature of a sacrament – a sign and instrument, that is, of communion with God and of unity with the human race'. We should reconsider this essential statement in the Constitution *Lumen gentium* (n. 1) so that our mission may derive full benefit from it. The face and function of the Church cannot be understood unless we go right to the depths of her nature: in conferring Baptism on us, she is our Mother, she gives us life in Christ, she makes us holy and transmits the gift of the Holy Spirit to us. In the Eucharist, a thank-offering to the Father and a bond of fellowship among us, we are privileged to share in Christ's redemptive sacrifice. Outside of this sacramental dimension, we cannot but have a superficial and totally perverted vision of the Church.

It seems to me that today there is a need to rekindle a love in Catholics for the Church which they form and which they should not view from the outside. The Church is no mere association; it is an authentic fellowship. To illustrate this concept, I want to quote St Irenaeus, the second-century Bishop of Lyons: 'The Father is above all, and he is the head of Christ, but the Word is through all things and he is himself the head of the Church; whilst the Spirit is in us all; and he is the living water which the Lord gave to those who believe in him and love him and know that there is one sole God and Father' (*Adversus haereses*, V,18,2). Aware of their dignity as responsible children in the bosom of the Christian family, the baptized can the better welcome the prophetic messages transmitted by the Church, the gift of the Faith and the moral rules that follow from it.[2]

'Feeling with the Church'

To possess and live the sense of the Church means first and foremost to believe in the God revealed by Jesus Christ and proclaimed by the Church.

In order to believe and, as disciples, to follow Jesus of Nazareth – the Son of God, the Lord, the Messiah, the Redeemer of the human race – we must first come to know him by continual meditation on Holy Scripture, and especially on the Gospel, where he speaks to us in the first person to present us with his personality, his message, his claims, his miracles, his passion, death and resurrection – that is, 'the mystery of his identity'.

To possess and live the sense of the Church means to know and love the Church and *sentire cum Ecclesia*; to know and love the Church who is 'in Christ, in the nature of a sacrament – a sign and instrument of communion with God and of unity with the whole human race' (*Lumen gentium* 1); who is the sheepfold, whose one and necessary door and whose Good Shepherd is Christ (John 10:1–10); who is the estate, the field of God, where Christ is the true vine making us who are its branches fruitful (John 15:1–5); who is the Body of Christ, in whom Christ's life is poured forth into us believers by the sacraments of the Faith; who is the New People of God, a people who has 'as its head Christ ... and its state is that of the dignity and freedom of the sons of God, in whose heart the Holy Spirit dwells as in a temple; its law, the new commandment to love as Christ loved us; its destiny, the kingdom of God' (*Lumen gentium* 9).

Of this Church we are members and children; by this Church we have been begotten to supernatural life in Baptism, which has grafted us into Christ. We should therefore love this Church as our Mother, because 'they cannot have God for Father who do not have the Church for Mother' (St Cyprian, *De Catholicae Ecclesiae unitate* 6; CSEL 3,1,214).

The Church is our Mother and Teacher: we ought filially and docilely to listen to what she says to us, to what she passes on to us and teaches us by means of the magisterium of the Successor of Peter, the perpetual and visible principle and foundation-stone of the unity of the Faith and of ecclesial communion, and of the Bishops who by divine institution have succeeded to the place of the Apostles as pastors of the Church. Whoever listens to them, listens to Christ; whoever despises them, despises Christ and the One who sent him (cf. Luke 10:6). Genuine Christians are always in tune with the magisterium of the Church; they accept it and, with God's help, put it into practice in the manifold circumstances of daily life. This is the meaning of *sentire cum Ecclesia*.[3]

The choice and mission of Peter

Jesus stated: 'On this rock I shall build my Church and the gates of hell will never prevail against her' (Matthew 16:18). The words attest Jesus' wish to build his Church with essential reference to the specific mission and power which he in his lifetime would confer on Simon. Jesus described Simon Peter as the foundation-stone on which the Church was going to be built. The relationship between Christ and Peter is thus reflected in the relationship between Peter and the Church. The former relationship charges the latter with importance and discloses its theological and spiritual significance which, objectively and ecclesially, is the basis of that jurisdiction.

Matthew is the only evangelist to record these words for us, but in this connection we should remember that Matthew is also the only one to have assembled material of particular interest about Peter (cf. Matthew 14:28–31), perhaps with those communities in mind for whom he was writing his Gospel and on whom he was keen to impress the new concept of 'the assembly summoned' in the name of Christ, present in Peter.

On the other hand, 'Peter', the new name which Jesus gives to Simon is confirmed by the other evangelists without any disagreement over the name's significance as explained by Matthew. Nor, for that matter, can one see what other meaning it could have.

We should also make clear that the 'Rock' of which Jesus is speaking is actually the person, Peter. Jesus says to him: '*Thou* art Kephas.' The context in which this is said allows us an even firmer grasp of the sense of that 'Thou' person. After Simon has said *who Jesus is* Jesus says *who Simon is*, in his plan for building the Church. True, Simon gets called 'Rock' after

34

making his profession of faith, and this implies a relationship between his faith and the role of *rock* conferred on him. But the quality of rock is attributed to Simon's person, not to one of his actions, even though it was very noble and pleasing to Jesus. The word 'rock' suggests something permanent and sound; hence it is applied to the person, rather than to an action of his, since by its nature an action would be transitory. Jesus' subsequent words confirm this, when he says that the gates of hell – that is, the powers of death – will never prevail 'against her'. The expression could refer to the Church or to the rock. Be that as it may, according to the logic of Christ's words, the Church founded on the rock can never be destroyed. The permanence of the Church is bound up with the rock. The relationship between Peter and the Church in itself duplicates the bond between the Church and Christ. For Jesus says '*my* Church'. Which means that the Church will always be *Christ's* Church, the Church belonging to Christ. She doesn't become Peter's Church. But, as Christ's Church, she is built on Peter, who is *Kephas*, in the name of and by the authority of Christ.

To Peter, Jesus says: 'Whatever you bind on earth will be bound in heaven; and whatever you loose on earth will be loosed in heaven' (Matthew 16:19). This is another metaphor used by Jesus to show that he wishes to invest Simon Peter with a complete and universal power guaranteed and ratified by heavenly approval. This is not only the power to enunciate points of doctrine or general directives to be acted upon; according to Jesus, it is the power 'to loose and to bind' – that is, to take all measures required for the life and development of the Church. The conjunction of the opposites 'to bind' and 'to loose' serves to show how total this power is.

We must, however, add at once that the purpose of this power is to give access to the Kingdom, not to close it: 'to open', to make it possible to enter the Kingdom of Heaven, and not to put obstacles in the way, which would be the same as 'closing' it. Such is the purpose of the Petrine ministry, rooted in the redemptive sacrifice of Christ, who came to save and to be the Door and Shepherd of all within the communion of the one sheepfold.[4]

The Bishop of Rome, the Successor of Peter

The Church is also Catholic in the sense that all of Christ's followers have to share in her world-wide mission of salvation by means of each individual apostolate. But the pastoral activity of all, and in particular the collegiate activity of the entire episcopate, attains unity through the *ministerium Petrinum* of the Bishop of Rome. 'The bishops,' says the Council, 'while loyally respecting the primacy and pre-eminence of their head, exercise their own proper authority for the good of their faithful, indeed for the good of the whole Church' (*Lumen gentium* 22). And we should add, again quoting the Council, that if the collegiate authority over the whole Church attains its particular expression in an ecumenical council, it is 'the prerogative of the Roman Pontiff to convoke such Councils, to preside over them and to confirm them' (*Lumen gentium* 22). Thus the Pope, the Bishop of Rome, is the head of all, as the principle of unity and communion.

For the Successor of Peter, it is not a matter of claiming powers such as those wielded by the earthly 'rulers' of whom Jesus speaks (cf. Matthew 20:25–28), but of being faithful to the will of the Church's Founder, who instituted this type of society and this mode of government to promote communion in faith and charity.

To respond to Christ's will, the Successor of Peter must, in a spirit of humble service and with the aim of assuring unity, assume and exercise the authority conferred on him. Even in the historically diverse ways of exercising it, he must imitate Christ in serving and reuniting those who are called to be part of the one fold. He will never subordinate to personal ends what he has received for Christ and for Christ's Church. He may never forget that the universal pastoral mission cannot but entail the deepest association with the Redeemer's sacrifice, with the mystery of the Cross.[5]

The doctrinal mission of the Successor of Peter

According to the Gospel texts, the universal pastoral mission of the Roman Pontiff, the Successor of Peter, involves a doctrinal mission. As the universal pastor, the Pope has a mission to announce revealed doctrine and to promote true faith in Christ throughout the Church. This is the integral meaning of the Petrine ministry.

The importance of the doctrinal mission entrusted to Peter – still according to Gospel sources – is due to the fact that he shares in the pastoral mission of Christ. Peter is the leader of those Apostles to whom Jesus said: 'As the Father sent me, so I am sending you' (John 20:21; cf. 17:18). As the universal pastor, Peter has to act on Christ's behalf and in tune with him throughout the vast human area in which Jesus wishes his Gospel to be preached and the saving truth to be carried – that is, the whole world. In the mission of universal pastor, the Successor of Peter is thus the heir to a doctrinal *munus*, in which he is intimately associated with Peter in Jesus' mission.

This detracts in no way from the pastoral mission of the Bishops who, according to the Second Vatican Council, have among their principal duties that of preaching the Gospel: for they 'are heralds of the faith ... who preach the faith to the people assigned to them, the faith which is destined to inform their thinking and direct their conduct' (*Lumen gentium* 25).

The Bishop of Rome, however, as the head of the episcopal college by Christ's will, is the first herald of the Faith, to whom falls the task of teaching revealed truth and of showing how it is to be applied in human behaviour. His is the primal responsibility for spreading the Faith in the world.

The Successor of Peter has carried out this doctrinal mission by issuing a continual series of oral and written interventions, which constitute the ordinary exercise of the Magisterium as the teaching of the truth to be believed and to be translated into practice (*fidem et mores*). The acts which express this Magisterium may be more or less frequent and may take differing forms, depending on the needs of the day, the requirements of particular situations, the possibilities and means available, and the methodologies and techniques of communication; but, given that they derive from an explicit or implicit intention to pronounce on matters of faith and morals, they are connected to the mandate received by Peter and invested with the authority conferred on him by Christ.

To discharge this task, the Successor of Peter, in personal form but with institutional authority, expresses the 'rule of the Faith', which all members of the Universal Church ought to keep – the faithful at large, catechists, teachers of religion, theologians – in seeking the meaning of the permanent contents of the Christian faith, or in relation to discussions that arise within and without the ecclesial community on various points or on the whole *corpus* of doctrine. True, everyone in the Church, and theologians especially, is called to carry out this task of constant clarification and explanation. But the mission of Peter and his successors is to establish and confirm what the Church has received and believed from the beginning, what the Apostles have taught, and what Holy Scripture and Christian tradition have fixed as the matter of faith and as the Christian norm of life. Furthermore, the other pastors of the Church, the Bishops who are the successors of the Apostles, are 'strengthened' by the Successor of Peter in their fellowship of faith with Christ and in the proper fulfilment of their mission. Thus the magisterium of the Bishop of Rome marks a line of charity and unity for all, which especially in times of maximum communication and discussion – such as our own – is absolutely necessary.

The Roman Pontiff has the mission of protecting Christians from errors in the field of faith and morals, and the duty of guarding the deposit of faith (cf. 2 Timothy 4:7). Woe to him if he were to fear being criticized or misunderstood. He is charged with bearing witness to Christ, to his word, to his law, to his love. To awareness of his own responsibility in the doctrinal and moral sphere, the Roman Pontiff must add the commitment of being, like Jesus, 'meek and humble of heart'.[6]

The priest and his ministry

First and foremost, the priest must be seen as the 'man of faith', since by virtue of his mission he has to convey the Faith by proclaiming the word. He cannot preach the Gospel convincingly if he has not deeply assimilated its message. He bears witness to the Faith by his actions and his whole life. Through his pastoral contacts he does his best to sustain his brothers and sisters in the Faith, to respond to their doubts and to strengthen them in their convictions.

Every priest should be prepared for his role as teacher of the Faith within the Christian community. Hence, in our seminaries, revealed doctrine needs to be taught in such a way that young men may understand what the object of their faith is, and may respond to the call from the Lord with a free, interiorized adherence to the Gospel message, assimilated in prayer.

As well as being the man of faith, the priest is also the 'man of the sacred', the witness to the Invisible, the spokesman of God revealed in Jesus Christ. The priest must be known as a man of God, a man of prayer, who is seen to pray, who is felt to pray. When he celebrates the Eucharist, when he hears confessions, when he anoints the sick or when he conducts funerals, gives blessings or holds prayer meetings, let him do this in a dignified way, taking the proper time and wearing the appropriate vestments.

Hence, the priest must nourish within himself a

spiritual life of high quality, inspired by the gift of his own ministerial priesthood. One may indeed speak of a 'spirituality of the diocesan priest'. His prayer life, his sharing, his efforts in life, are inspired by his apostolic activity, which is nourished by a life lived wholly with God. It has been observed that a time of intense pastoral activity often coincides with a period which is strong in spiritual life. The Second Vatican Council has reminded us, moreover, of 'that love of God and man, which is the soul of the apostolate' (*Lumen gentium* 33).

The priest is the man of faith, man of the sacred, and also the 'man of communion'. He it is who assembles the People of God and strengthens their unity by means of the Eucharist; he is the leading spirit of brotherly love among all.

The priest cannot venture on his own on the labour awaiting him in the Lord's vineyard. He operates with his brothers in the priesthood. He collaborates with his own bishop. He does his best to forge brotherly links between members of the priestly college; in the presbyteral group especially, spiritual friendship is a great stimulus to ministry. The priest, furthermore, unites the members of the People of God who are entrusted to his pastoral care.[7]

Priestly celibacy: its meaning and value

Following the example of Christ the Lord himself, apostolic teaching and all relevant tradition, the

Latin Church has willed and continues to will, that all those who receive the sacrament of Order embrace this renunciation for the Kingdom of Heaven. This tradition, however, includes respect for the different traditions of other Churches. For this tradition is a characteristic, a peculiarity and a heritage of the Catholic Latin Church, to which she owes much and in which she is determined to persist – despite all the difficulties to which fidelity of this kind could be exposed and despite the various symptoms of weakness and crisis displayed by individual priests. We are all aware that 'we have this treasure in vessels of clay'; all the same, we know very well that it is a treasure indeed.

The priest, by his celibacy, becomes the 'man for others' in a different way from someone who gets married and as husband and father likewise becomes a 'man for others', chiefly within his own family circle – that is, for his wife and, with her, for the children they bring into the world.

In renouncing the fatherhood enjoyed by a husband, the priest seeks another fatherhood and, as it were, another motherhood, remembering the Apostle's words about the children to whom he painfully gives birth. They are the children of his spirit, the people whom the Good Shepherd has entrusted to his care.

There are many, many more of these people than any ordinary human family could contain. The pastoral vocation is great, and the Council teaches that it is universal; it is directed to the whole Church and it is therefore also a missionary vocation. Usually it is linked to the service of a particular community of God's People, each member of which has a claim on the priest's attention, care and love. To be available for such service, for such care and love, the priest's heart must be free.

Celibacy is the sign of a freedom to be of service. By virtue of this sign, the hierarchical priesthood, otherwise called 'ministerial', is, according to the tradition of the Roman Church, more strictly 'ordained' than the common priesthood of the faithful.

Committed to maintaining the celibacy of priests as a special gift for the Kingdom of God, the Church professes her faith and expresses her hope in her Master, Redeemer and Spouse, and also in Him who is the 'Lord of the harvest' and 'giver of the gift'. For, 'all that is perfect is given us from above and comes down from the Father of light' (James 1:17). Let us not weaken this faith and trust by our human doubts or our faint-heartedness.[8]

The laity in the Church

The laity form a living, active and responsible part of the Church, and this accords with the will of Jesus Christ, who wished his Church to be open to all.

Suffice it here to recall the behaviour of the owner of the vineyard in the very significant and thought-provoking parable told by Jesus. Seeing some unemployed people, the owner said to them: 'You go to my vineyard too' (Matthew 20:4). 'From that distant day,' comments the 1987 Synod of Bishops, 'the call has never failed to resound throughout history; it is addressed to every person who comes into this world ... The call not only concerns Pastors, clergy, and men and women religious. It is addressed to everyone; lay people as well are personally called by the Lord, from whom they receive a mission on behalf of the Church and the world' (*Christifideles laici*, 2). All are invited 'to let themselves be reconciled with God' (2 Corinthians 5:20), to let themselves be saved and to co-operate in universal salvation, since God 'wants everyone to be saved' (1 Timothy 2:4). All are invited, with their own personal qualities, to labour in the Father's 'vineyard', where each has a personal place and a personal reward.

The laity's calling entails their participation in the Church's life and consequently their intimate communion in Christ's own life too. It is a divine gift and at the same time a mutual commitment. For didn't Jesus ask the disciples who had followed him to remain constantly united with him and in him, and to let his own living energy burst into their minds and hearts? 'Remain in me, as I in you. Without me you can do nothing' (John 15:4–5). As for priests, so for the laity: true fruitfulness depends on union with Christ.'

The Church is holy and all her members are called to

be holy. The laity share in the holiness of the Church, being full members of the Christian community: and this sharing (which we may call ontological) in the Church's holiness is translated, in the laity's case, into an individual ethical commitment to sanctification. In this capacity for and vocation to holiness, all members of the Church are equal (cf. Galatians 3:28).

The degree of personal holiness doesn't depend on the position one holds in society, least of all in the Church, but only on the degree of charity one practises (cf. 1 Corinthians 13). A member of the laity who open-heartedly welcomes God's love into his or her heart and life is holier than any priest or bishop who only welcomes it half-heartedly.[10]

The prayer life of every Christian, and therefore of all members of the laity, cannot thrive without participation in the Liturgy, recourse to the sacrament of Reconciliation and above all the celebration of the Eucharist, where sacramental communion with Christ is the source of that kind of mutual immanence between the soul and Christ which he foretells: 'Whoever eats my flesh and drinks my blood lives in me and I live in that person' (John 6:56). The eucharistic banquet assures the Christian of that spiritual nourishment which makes it possible to produce much fruit. So the *Christifideles laici* are also called and invited to an intense Eucharistic life. For them, sacramental participation in Sunday Mass should be the source of their spiritual life and also of their apostolate. Blessed are they who, besides Sunday Mass and Communion, feel drawn and prompted to frequent Communion, recommended by so many of the Saints, especially in recent times, when the apostolate of the laity has been developing more and more.[11]

The Christian laity as 'children of the promise' are called to bear witness in the world to the greatness and fruitfulness of the hope they bear in their hearts: a hope based on the teaching and work of Jesus Christ, who died and rose again for the salvation of all. In a world which, despite appearances to the contrary, is often racked with anguish over the ever-renewed and disappointing experience of the limitations, inadequacies and even emptiness of many structures created to ensure human happiness on earth, their witness of hope is particularly needed to direct spirits in their quest for a future life, beyond the relative values of the things of this world. In this, the laity as workers in the service of the Gospel 'through the structures of secular life', have a special relevance of their own. They show that Christian hope does not mean shunning the world, nor renunciation of a full realization of earthly existence, but an opening of it to the transcendental dimension of life eternal, which alone gives this existence its true value.[12]

Women's role in the Church

In the context of Christian anthropology, every human person has his or her dignity; and as persons women have no less dignity than men. Too often, women are regarded as objects because of male egoism, of which there have been endless manifestations in the past and of which there are still many today. In today's situation there are all sorts of cultural and social reasons for this, and these need calm and objective consideration. Even so, it is not hard to detect the influence of a tendency to domination and arrogance, a tendency which has found and is still finding its victims especially among women and young girls. However, the phenomenon has been and still is more general than this, having its origins (as I wrote in *Christifideles laici*) 'in that unjust and deleterious mentality which considers the human being as a thing, as an object to buy and sell, as an instrument for selfish interests or for pleasure only' (n. 49).

The Christian laity are called to fight against all the forms which this mentality takes, including advertising, which is motivated by the intention to accelerate the frenetic race for consumer goods. But women themselves have a duty to play their part in obtaining respect for their personality, by not lowering themselves to any form of complicity with anything which militates against their dignity.

Perfection for women does not mean being like men, masculinizing themselves until they lose their specifically womanly qualities. Their perfection – with its self-affirmation and relative autonomy – is to be women, equal to men but different. In civil society and in the Church too, the fact that women are equal and different has to be recognized.

Difference does not mean an inevitable and almost implacable opposition. In the Bible story of the creation, co-operation between man and woman is laid down as the condition for the development of the human race and for its work of mastering the universe: 'Be fruitful, multiply, fill the earth and subdue it' (Genesis 1:28). In the light of this command from the Creator, the Church holds that 'the married couple and the family constitute the first and basic expression of the social dimension of the faithful' (*Christifideles laici* 40). On a more general plane we may say that the renewal of the temporal order can only come about by the co-operation of men and women.[13]

Women have understanding, sensitive, compassionate hearts, giving them a tactful and practical approach to charity. In the Church, we know, there have always been many women – religious and lay, mothers of families and single women – who have devoted their lives to alleviating human suffering. What wonderful pages they have contributed to the annals of dedication to the needs of the poor, the sick, the infirm, the paralyzed, and all those rejected by society, both in former times and in today's world. How many names leap from heart to lips when we only intend to make a passing mention of those heroic figures who exercised charity with a tact and skill entirely feminine, be it within the family or in Institutes, in hospitals or in dealing with people vulnerable to moral anguish, oppression or exploitation. Nothing of this escapes God's eye, and the Church too treasures the names and exemplary activities of those many, many noble representatives of charity; sometimes she enters them in the register of her Saints.

A significant field for the female apostolate in the Church is that of contributing to the Liturgy. Women's attendance at church services, where they usually outnumber the men, shows their commitment to the Faith, their spiritual sensitivity, their inclination to piety and their attachment to liturgical prayer and the Eucharist.

In this co-operation of women with the priest and other members of the faithful in the eucharistic celebration, we may see a type of the Virgin Mary's co-operation with Christ in the Incarnation and the Redemption. *Ecce ancilla Domini*: 'Behold the handmaid of the Lord; be it unto me according to your word' (Luke 1:38). Mary is the model of Christian womanhood, spreading the mystery of the incarnate and redeeming Word through the world.

The true promotion of women consists in promoting them to that which is proper to them and suited to them as women – that is, as creatures different from men, called, no less than men, to be a model of human personality. This is 'emancipation' as indicated and intended by Jesus, who wished to assign women a mission of their own, appropriate to their natural difference from men. Discharging this mission allows women to develop their personalities and thus to serve humanity, and particularly the Church, in a way consistent with their qualities.[14]

Quite recently and even in Catholic circles, a claim has been advanced by some women to be admitted to the *priestly ministry*. The claim is in fact based on a false assumption. For the ministerial priesthood is not a job which one can take on the basis of social qualification or legal procedures, but only in obedience to the will of Christ. Now, Jesus entrusted the task of the ministerial priesthood to members of the male sex alone. In spite of having also invited certain women to follow him and in spite of having asked them to work with him, he did not call or admit any of them to the group whom he had entrusted with the ministerial priesthood of his Church. His will is made plain by the sum of his behaviour, as also by significant actions, which Christian tradition has always interpreted as pointers to be followed.

Thus we see from the Gospel that Jesus never sent women on preaching missions, as he did the group of the Twelve, who were all men (cf. Luke 9:1–6);

similarly with the Seventy-Two, among whom no female presence is mentioned (cf. Luke 10:1-20).

Only to the Twelve does Jesus give authority over the Kingdom: 'Now I confer a kingdom on you, just as my Father conferred one on me' (Luke 22:29). Only on the Twelve does he confer the mission and power of repeating the Eucharist on his behalf (cf. Luke 22:19). Only to the Apostle does he give the power to remit sins (cf. John 20:22-23) and to undertake the work of universal evangelization (cf. Matthew 28:18-20; Mark 16:16-18).

Christ's will was followed by the Apostles and by those subsequently responsible for the earliest communities, thus giving rise to the Christian tradition which has been in force in the Church ever since. I felt it my duty to confirm this tradition in my Apostolic Letter *Ordinatio sacerdotalis* (22 May 1994), declaring that 'the Church has no power whatever to confer priestly ordination on women, and that this ruling should be held as definitive by all the Church's faithful' (n. 4). Here faithfulness to the pastoral ministry as instituted by Christ is at stake.[15]

The relationship between the Magisterium and theology

The Church particularly needs her theologians in this day and age, which is so deeply marked by radical change in every sphere of life and society. The Bishops of the Church, to whom our Lord has entrusted the task of preserving the unity of the Faith and the proclamation of the message – individually for their dioceses and collegially with Peter's Successor for the Universal Church – all need your work as theologians, your dedication and the fruit of your reflections. We want to hear you and are eager to receive the great help which your training as responsible scientists can be to us.

But this authentic theological training and, by the same token, your teaching of theology cannot be sound and fruitful unless you concentrate on what inspires it and where it comes from – that is to say, the word of God contained in Sacred Scripture and the Sacred Tradition of the Church, as interpreted by the authentic Magisterium down the ages (cf. *Dei verbum* 10). True academic freedom must be seen in relation to the final purpose of academic work, which looks to the total truth of the human person. The theologian's contribution will only enrich the Church if it takes into proper account the proper function of Bishops and the rights of the faithful. To Bishops, theology attributes the duty of safeguarding Christian authenticity, the unity of the Faith and moral instruction, in accordance with the Apostle Paul's exhortations: 'Proclaim the message and, welcome or unwelcome, insist on it. Refute falsehood, correct error,' recall to obedience ... It is the right of the faithful not to be disturbed by theories and hypotheses on which they are not qualified to pass judgement, or which can easily be simplified or manipulated by public opinion for purposes remote from the truth. On the day he died, John Paul I stated: 'Among the rights of the faithful, one of the greatest is to receive the word of God in all its entirety and purity ...' (28 September 1979). It is right that the theologian should be free, but that freedom should be an openness to the truth and light that come from faith and from loyalty to the Church.[16]

The Church wants theological research to be independent and not identified with the Church's magisterium, but to recognize that, with the magisterium, it is committed in common service to the truth of the Faith and to the People of God. That tensions and even conflicts will arise cannot be ruled out. But this cannot be ruled out either regarding relations between the Church and science. The reason for this is to be found in the finite nature of the human mind, which is limited in its scope and therefore open to error. Nonetheless, we can always hope for a reconciliatory solution, if we take our stand precisely on the ability of the human mind to reach the truth.[17]

Theology is a science with all the potentialities of human knowledge. It is free as to the way it applies its methods and analyses. Yet, theology must be mindful of the relationship in which it stands to the Church. We do not owe the Faith to ourselves; it is 'founded on the Apostles, and Christ himself is the corner-stone' (Ephesians 2:20). Even theology has to presuppose the Faith. It can clarify and promote it, but it cannot produce it. Even theology must always stand on the shoulders of the Fathers in the Faith. It knows that its specific sphere doesn't consist of dates and historical facts in a *vas clusum*, but rather of the living Faith of the Church. So theologians teach on behalf of and by the mandate of the Church – that is, of the communion of faith. They can and should put forward new suggestions for understanding the Faith, but these are only offered to the Church at large. Many corrections and adaptations are needed before the Church at large can accept them.

Theology is a very disinterested service to the community of believers, in the deepest sense, for it essentially entails objective discussion, brotherly dialogue, openness and a readiness to change its own opinion.

Believers have the right to know how far they can go regarding the Faith. Theology should show us where to call a halt. The magisterium intervenes only to state the truth of God's word, above all when this is threatened by distortions and false interpretations. In this context too is to be seen the infallibility of the Church's magisterium.

Love for the institutional Church, which also involves loyalty to the witness of faith and to the Church's magisterium, does not distract theologians from their work, nor does it take away any of their inalienable independence. Magisterium and theology each have a different task. Hence neither can diminish the other. Both of them serve the same cause. Precisely because they are so linked, constant dialogue has to be maintained between them. In the years since the Council there have been many examples of good collaboration between theology and magisterium. Strengthen this foundation and, even though new conflicts will probably arise, go on with your common work in the spirit of the common Faith, of that same hope and the love that unites us all.[18]

This studying of theology, here and everywhere in the Church, is thinking about the Faith, and thinking within the Faith. A theology that doesn't deepen faith, that doesn't lead to prayer, may discourse eloquently about God; but the discourse can never be truly about God, the Living God, the God who Is, and whose Being is Love. From this it follows that theology can be authentic only within the Church, within the community of faith. Only when the teaching of theologians conforms to the teaching of the Bishops united with the Pope, can the People of God know with certainty that this teaching is 'the faith which has been once and for all entrusted to the saints' (Jude 3).

This is no limitation for theologians but a liberation, since it preserves them from changes in fashion and keeps them safely bound to Christ's unchangeable truth, the truth that sets us free (John 7:32).[19]

Catechesis and orthodoxy

Christians today must be formed to live in a world which largely ignores God or which, in religious matters, in place of an exacting and fraternal dialogue, stimulating for all, too often flounders in a debasing indifferentism, if not maintaining a scornful attitude of suspicion in the name of the progress it has made in the field of scientific 'explanations'. To 'hold on' in this world, to offer to all a 'dialogue of salvation' in which each person feels respected in his or her most basic dignity – the dignity of one who is seeking God – we need a catechesis which trains the young people and adults of our communities to remain clear and consistent in their faith, to affirm serenely their Christian and Catholic identity, to 'see him who is invisible' and to adhere so firmly to the absoluteness of God that they can be witnesses to him in a materialistic civilization that denies him.

Without monopolizing or enforcing uniformity, the parish remains the pre-eminent place for catechesis. It must rediscover its vocation, which is to be a fraternal and welcoming family home, where those who have been baptized and confirmed become aware of forming the People of God. In that home, the bread of good doctrine and the Eucharistic Bread are broken for them in abundance, in the setting of the one act of worship; from that home they are sent out day by day to their apostolic mission in all the centres of activity in the life of the world.

Family catechesis precedes, accompanies and enriches all other forms of catechesis. Furthermore, in places where anti-religious legislation endeavours even to prevent education in the Faith, and in places where widespread unbelief or invasive secularism makes real religious growth practically impossible, 'the Church of the home' remains the one place where children and young people can receive an authentic catechesis.

Thus there cannot be too great an effort on the part of Christian parents to prepare for this ministry of being their own children's catechists and to carry it out with tireless zeal. Encouragement must also be given to the individuals or institutions that, through person-to-person contacts, through meetings and through all kinds of pedagogical means, help parents to perform their task; the service they are doing to catechesis is beyond price.[20]

The Church and art

Art too in all its manifestations – and to these must be added the potential offered by the cinema and television – has humanity as its fundamental theme: the human image, human truth. Though appearance may often be to the contrary, even contemporary art is cognizant of these deep-down assertions and demands. The religious and Christian origin of art is by no means exhausted. Themes such as guilt and grace, deceit and liberation, injustice and justice, compassion and freedom, solidarity with and love for one's neighbour, hope and consolation, all have their place in today's literature, in text-books and film scripts, and get ample feed-back.

Collaboration between the Church and art regarding humanity is based on the fact that both seek to set humanity free from slavery and want it to become self-aware. They open the way to freedom for humanity: freedom from the pressures of needs, of productivity at any cost, of efficiency, of programming and functionalism.[21]

The Church and the dignity of the person

Man has been compelled to submit to a conception of reality imposed on him by coercion, and not reached by virtue of his own reason and the exercise of his own freedom. This principle must be overturned and total recognition must be given to the rights of the human conscience, which is bound only to the truth, both natural and revealed. The recognition of these rights represents the primary foundation of every authentically free political order.

No one can consider himself extraneous or indifferent to the lot of another member of the human family. No one can say that he is not responsible for the well-being of his brother or sister (cf. Genesis 4:9; Luke 10:29–37; Matthew 25:31–46).

Since it is not an ideology, the Christian faith does not presume to imprison changing socio-political realities in a rigid schema, and it recognizes that human life is realized in history in conditions that are diverse and imperfect. Furthermore, in constantly reaffirming the transcendent dignity of the person, the Church's method is always that of respect for freedom.

But freedom attains its full development only by accepting the truth. In a world without truth, freedom loses its foundation and man is exposed to the violence of passion and to manipulation, both open and hidden. The Christian upholds freedom and serves it, constantly offering to others the truth which he has known (cf. John 8:31–32), in accordance with the missionary nature of his vocation. While paying heed to every fragment of truth which he encounters in the life experience and in the culture of individuals and of nations, he will not fail to affirm in dialogue with others all that his faith and the correct use of reason have enabled him to understand.

Man's principal resource is man himself. His intelligence enables him to discover the earth's productive potential and the many ways in which human needs can be satisfied. It is his disciplined work in close collaboration with others that makes possible the creation of ever more extensive working communities which can be relied on to transform man's natural and human environments.[22]

The Church in the service of truth and charity

The work of building up the Body of Christ has been entrusted to all of us in the Church. Today a vital demand for *evangelization* certainly exists. This can take a variety of forms. There are many ways of serving the Gospel. Despite scientific and technological progress, which actually reflects a sort of human co-operation in God's creative work, the Faith is challenged and even directly opposed by ideologies and life-styles recognizing neither God nor the moral law.

The fundamental human and Christian values are put in question by criminality, violence and terrorism. Honesty and justice in the work-place and in public life are often violated. All over the world vast sums are being spent on armaments, while millions of poor people struggle for the barest necessities of life. Alcoholism and drug addiction lay a heavy tribute on the individual and on society. The commercial exploitation of sex through pornography is an insult to human dignity and a danger to the future of the young. Family life is being subjected to strong pressures, now that many people mistakenly regard fornication, adultery, divorce and contraception as acceptable. Unborn children are cruelly put to death, and the lives of the aged are gravely endangered by a mentality that would be happy to fling wide the door to euthanasia.

Faced with all this, the Christian faithful should not allow themselves to be discouraged, nor should they conform to the spirit of the world. On the contrary, they are called to recognize the supremacy of God and of his law, to make their voices heard and to unite their efforts on behalf of moral values, to set society an example by their own right conduct and to help the needy. Christians are called to act, in the serene conviction that grace is more powerful than sin, thanks to the victory of the Cross of Christ.[23]

Christ's Cross has bought us freedom from the slavery of sin and death. This freedom, this liberation, is so fundamental and all-embracing as to demand a freedom from all the other forms of slavery which are bound up with the introduction of sin into the world. This liberation insists that we struggle against poverty. And it requires all who belong to Christ to commit themselves to making tenacious efforts to alleviate the sufferings of the poor. Yes, the Church's evangelizing mission includes energetic and sustained action to achieve justice, peace and over-all human development. Not to perform these tasks would be to fail in the work of evangelization; it would be to betray the example set by Christ, who came 'to bring good news to the poor' (Luke 4:18); it would in fact be to reject the results of the Incarnation, in which 'the Word became flesh' (John 2:14).[24]

Like a good mother, the Church loves everyone: children, young people, the aged, workers, the homeless, the starving, the handicapped, those who suffer in spirit, and those who acknowledge their sins and so, through her, experience the healing touch of Christ. To such, but particularly to the poor, the Church offers the Good News of the human and supernatural dignity of the human person. In Christ, we have been raised to the state of children of God. We are God's children, called to live in dignity in this world and destined to eternal life.

The Church is the home of poor and rich alike, 'for there is no favouritism with God' (Galatians 2:6). Yet each community in the Church should make a particular effort to make the poor feel absolutely at home in it.[25]

The Church demonstrates her vitality through the broadness of her charity. There can be no greater disaster for her than for her love to grow weak. The Church should spare no efforts in demonstrating her compassion for the neediest and for all victims of pain, by alleviating their sufferings, by serving them and by helping them to give a salvific meaning to their sufferings.[26]

The Church and culture

Thought about culture has a long history in the life of the Church. Indeed, it has been a constant preoccupation, becoming remarkably accentuated at crucial moments of human history. We are in fact considering a topic which is central to human life and the life of the Church.

Culture is primarily to do with human beings and the meaning of their existence. I said as much in my address to UNESCO some years ago: 'For a culture to be created, man has to be seen – integrally and in its remotest consequences – as an autonomous, particular value, a subject endowed with transcendence of person. We must affirm man for himself, and not for other motives or reasons: for himself alone! Even more, we must love man because he is man, we must insist on love for man because of the particular dignity that is his' (Address to UNESCO, 2 June 1980, n. 10). A culture should be a space and a tool for making human life ever more humane (cf. *Redemptor hominis* 14; *Gaudium et Spes* 38), so that people can lead decent lives in accordance with God's plan. A culture which is not at the service of the human person is no true culture.

In attempting to evangelize our culture, then, the Church makes a radical option for humanity. Her option is thus for a true, integral humanism, raising the dignity of humanity to its true and inalienable dimension of the children of God. Christ reveals humanity to itself (cf. *Gaudium et Spes* 22), and restores people's greatness and dignity to them by letting them rediscover the value of their humanity, though obscured by sin. What immense value human beings must have in God's eyes, to have deserved so great a Redeemer!

Consequently, the Church's activities cannot be associated with those of the types of 'humanism' which limit themselves to a merely economic, biological or psychological view of human nature. The Christian conception of life is always open to God's love. Faithful to her aforesaid vocation, the Church holds herself above the various ideologies, so as to opt uniquely for man on the basis of the liberating Christian message.

This humanistic option from the Christian point of view requires clear awareness of a scale of values, since these are the foundations of every society. Without values there is no chance of building a truly humane society; for these determine not only the course of our personal lives, but that of the politics and strategies of public life as well. A culture that ceases to be founded on the supreme values inevitably turns against humanity.

The big problems afflicting contemporary culture originate from this desire to isolate private and public life from a correct scale of values. No economic or political model will fully serve the common good if it is not based on the fundamental values corresponding to the truth about the human person, 'the truth which has been revealed to us by Christ in all its fullness and depth' (*Dives in misericordia* 1,2). Systems that regard economics as the unique and determining factor of the social fabric are doomed, by their own internal logic, to turn against humanity.[27]

The Church and the State

The Christian message brings glad tidings for everyone: for the political, economic and legal world too. When the authority of the Church, within the sphere of her own mission, proclaims Christian doctrine or gives rulings *of a moral nature* on matters in the political order, and when she encourages promotion of the dignity and inalienable rights of man, she is, above all, seeking the integral good of the body politic and, ultimately, the integral good of the individual. The Church, at the same time, recognizes that it is the duty of the Catholic laity, when faced with questions susceptible of various solutions in the vast field of politics, to find such solutions as are compatible with Gospel values. In union with all those people wishing to promote the good of the community, they bear a great responsibility: for seeking and applying truly humane solutions to the challenge posed by modern times and social coexistence. The Church shares in the best of human aspirations and offers mankind what she has herself: 'A global perspective on man and human realities' (*Populorum progressio* 13).

Both Church and State, each in its own domain and with its own means, are at the service of man's personal and social vocation. Thus ample room opens up for dialogue and for various kinds of co-operation, based always on mutual respect for the identity of each and for the functions proper to each of these two institutions. The Church recognizes, respects and encourages the legitimate autonomy of temporal and specifically political affairs. Her mission is set on a different plane. She is 'the sign and the safeguard of the transcendental dimension of the human person' (*Gaudium et Spes* 76).[28]

In no way is the Church to be confused with the political community, nor is she tied to any political system (*Gaudium et Spes* 76). Even less is she to be identified with any party, and it would be deplorable if individuals and institutions, of whatever stamp they may be, were tempted to make use of her for their own particular advantage. Such an attitude would reveal an ignorance of the nature and real mission of the Church and would involve a lack of respect for the aims she has received from her Divine Founder.

But, this said, we should not conclude that the message of salvation entrusted to the Church has nothing to say to the body politic in order to enlighten it with the Gospel. To the Church it pertains, as the Council teaches, 'to carry out her task among men without hindrance, and to pass moral judgements even in matters relating to politics, whenever the fundamental rights of man or the salvation of souls requires it' (*Gaudium et Spes* 76). So it is not a question of undue interference in a field to which she is a stranger, but of a service offered, for love of Jesus Christ, to the whole community, and prompted by a desire to contribute to the common good, encouraged by the Lord's words: 'The truth will make you free' (John 8:32).[29]

Holy yet sinful

We have to acknowledge that, the Church also being a community made up of sinners, there has been no lack over the centuries of transgressions against the law of love. I mean the failures of individuals and groups sporting the name of Christian, on the plane of mutual relations, whether of the order of person to person, or of social and international dimensions. That is the sorry fact, found in the history of men and nations, and in Church history too. Aware of their true vocation to love following Christ's example, Christians humbly and penitently confess those offences against love, yet without ceasing to believe in the love that, according to St Paul, 'endures whatever comes' and 'will never come to an end' (1 Corinthians 13:7–8). But if the history of mankind and of the Church abounds in sins against charity which grieve and sadden us, we must at the same time joyfully and gratefully recognize that throughout the Christian centuries there has never been a lack of marvellous witness on behalf of love, and that many a time – as well we remember – the witness borne has been heroic.[30]

III

PRAYER

First of all, we should pray
because we are believers,
for prayer is the recognition
of our limitations and of our dependence:
from God we come, to God we belong,
to God we shall return.

*Prayer is the personal dialogue of the 'individual'
and the 'community' with God. To be authentic,
prayer must be theologically exact; for prayer is a
spiritual contact with the Infinite and with the
Absolute, and we know that God has revealed himself in Christ and that Jesus Christ is present in the
Church which he has willed and founded.*

*Prayer is always prayer of adoration, prayer of
atonement and prayer of petition: Jesus as Man is the
first and supreme intercessor; he prays to the Father
on behalf of the entire human race. And since adoration is the highest form of prayer, and since sacrifice
is the supreme manifestation of adoration, Jesus*

does away with all forms of sacrificial worship, including the Jewish sacrifice of the Paschal Lamb, and offers himself as the unique, everlasting and universal Sacrifice by dying on the Cross.

Jesus purposely instituted the Eucharist at the end of the Jewish Passover supper to signify that, the sacrifice of the lamb being abolished for ever, he alone would be the true and only Lamb to be sacrificed as the highest and universal expression of adoration, and he purposely makes himself 'really and substantially' present under the Species of Bread and Wine – that is to say, as Victim – to commemorate the real sacrifice of the Cross, in which his Body was really killed and his Blood was truly shed.

For this reason, authentic prayer is that which is expressly willed by God by means of Revelation and the Redemption: prayer takes place 'through Christ, with Christ and in Christ' and is completely expressed by Holy Mass which, by the priest at the altar, mystically but really represents the Sacrifice of the Cross.

All other prayers and devotions have their source in Holy Mass and lead back to it. To attend Holy Mass is to find oneself back on Calvary and in the Upper Room.

Why and how to pray

First of all, we should pray because we are believers. For prayer is the recognition of our limitations and of our dependence; from God we come, to God we belong, to God we shall return! Hence the least we can do is surrender ourselves to him, our Creator and Lord, in full and total trust. Some people assert and do their best to prove that the universe is eternal and that all the order we observe in the universe – human beings with their brain-power and freedom included – has only come about by chance. Scientific studies and the experience of many honest people, however, say that these ideas, despite being asserted and even taught, have not been proved and invariably leave those who hold them anxious and confused, since they are very well aware that any object in motion must have had a push from outside! They are very well aware that chance cannot produce the perfect order existing in the universe and in the human entity! Everything is marvellously ordered, from the infinitessimal particles making up the atom, to the galaxies that wheel around in space! Everything points to a plan comprehending every manifestation of nature, from inert matter to human thought. Where there is order, there is intelligence, and where there is a supreme order, there is the supreme Intelligence whom we call 'God' and whom Jesus has revealed to us as Love and taught us to call 'Father'.

So, by reflecting on the nature of the universe and

on our own lives, we understand and acknowledge that we are creatures, limited yet sublime, who owe our nature to the Infinite Majesty of the Creator! This being so, prayer is, before all else, an act of intelligence, a feeling of humility and thankfulness, an attitude of trust and surrender to him who has lovingly given us life. Prayer is a mysterious but nonetheless real dialogue with God, a dialogue of confidence and love.

However, we are Christians and so we ought to pray like Christians. Now, for the Christian, prayer takes on a particular character which totally changes its innermost nature and innermost value. Christians are disciples of Jesus; we truly believe Jesus to be the Incarnate Word, the Son of God, come to dwell among us on earth.

When Jesus was on earth, his life was one ceaseless prayer, a continuous act of adoration and love addressed to the Father; and since the highest form of prayer is sacrifice, the climax of our Lord's prayer life was the sacrifice of the Cross, anticipated in the Eucharist at the Last Supper and handed down in Holy Mass for all ages to come.

So Christians know that their prayer life is Jesus; all our prayer lives start from Jesus; it is he who prays within us, with us, for us. All who believe in God pray; but Christians pray in Jesus Christ. Christ is our prayer!

The highest form of prayer is Holy Mass because,

in Holy Mass, Jesus himself is really present, renewing the sacrifice of the Cross. But every prayer is valuable, especially the 'Our Father', which Christ himself was pleased to teach the Apostles and everybody on earth.

In uttering the words of the 'Our Father', Jesus created a practical model and universal synthesis. For everything one can and should say to the Father is contained in those seven petitions which we all know by heart. In them is such simplicity that even a child can learn them; but at the same time there is such depth that one might spend a lifetime reflecting on their meaning.

A further reason why we should pray is that we are frail and guilty. Humbly and realistically we need to admit that we are poor creatures, confused in our ideas, tempted to wrong-doing, frail and weak, constantly in need of inner strengthening and consolation. Prayer gives us strength for high ideals, for keeping the Faith, for charity, purity and generosity. Prayer gives us the courage to rise above indifference, or above guilt, if we have been unlucky enough to yield to temptation and weakness. Prayer gives us the light to see and consider events in our personal lives and in history itself in the salvific perspective of God and eternity.

So you must not stop praying! Let no day go by without praying a little! Prayer is a duty; it is also a great joy, since it is a dialogue with God through

Jesus Christ. Every Sunday, Holy Mass and, if you possibly can, sometimes on a weekday as well; every day, prayers in the morning and at night, and whenever else you can find a moment!

St Paul wrote to the early Christians as follows: 'Be persevering in your prayers' (Colossians 4:2); 'With every sort of prayer and entreaty, keep praying on every possible occasion' (Ephesians 6:18).[1]

Perseverance in prayer

If you really wish to follow Christ, if you want your love for him to grow and last, you must be *diligent in prayer*. This is the key to the vitality of your life in Christ. Without prayer, your faith and your love will die. If you are constant in daily prayer and in attendance at Sunday Mass, your love for Jesus will grow. And your heart will know such joy and deep peace as the world could never give you.[2]

Nourish your day with as much prayer as you can and allowing for moments of particular intimacy with the Lord, whether individually or in a group. Only prolonged contact with him can transform each of us inwardly into a disciple of his. Only by being nourished by long hours of prayer, meditation, concentration and silent listening to God, will a believer be able to speak to other people about the Divine Mystery, to hand it on and to bear witness to it in the presence of others.[3]

The Gospel reminds us of 'the need to pray continually and never lose heart' (Luke 18:1). So every day, devote a little while to conversing with God, as proof of the fact that you sincerely love him; for love always seeks to be close to the beloved. This is why prayer must come before everything else; people who do not take this view, who do not put this into practice, cannot plead the excuse of being short of time; what they are short of is love.[4]

The Eucharist, the core of Christian life

From the Eucharist we all receive the grace and strength for everyday life, for living a truly Christian existence, in the joy of knowing that God loves us, that Christ has died for us and that the Holy Spirit lives in us.

Our full participation in the Eucharist is the true source of that Christian spirit we should like to see in our own lives and in every aspect of society. Wherever we work – in politics, in the economy, in culture, in the social or scientific fields – it does not matter what our job may be – the Eucharist is a challenge to our daily lives.

There must always be consistency between what we believe and what we do. We cannot live on the glories of our Christian past. Our union with Christ in the Eucharist must be manifest in the truth of our lives today: in our actions, in our sense of values, in our life-style, in our relationships with others.

For each of us the Eucharist is a summons to make an ever greater effort to live as true followers of Christ: truthful in what we say, generous in what we do, caring for and respectful of the dignity and rights of all, whatever their class or their income may be; ready to make personal sacrifices, loyal and just, generous, prudent, compassionate and self-disciplined; aiming at the good of our families, of our young people, of our country, of Europe, of the world. The truth of our union with Christ in the Eucharist is attested by whether or not we truly love our neighbour, whoever that may be, and by the way we treat other people, especially our own families: husbands and wives, children and parents, brothers and sisters. It is attested by the effort we really make to be reconciled with our enemies, to forgive those who wrong us or offend us.[5]

Given the agnostic society – a sadly hedonistic and permissive one – in which we live, it is essential to deepen our teaching on the august Mystery of the Eucharist, in such a way as to acquire and maintain absolute certainty over the nature and purpose of the Sacrament which is rightly called the core of the Christian message and of the life of the Church. The Eucharist is the mystery of mysteries; so its acceptance means totally accepting the nexus 'Christ-and-the-Church', from the preambles of the Faith to the doctrine of the Redemption, to the concept of sacrifice and of consecrated priesthood, to the dogma of 'transubstantiation', to the importance of legislation in liturgical matters.

Today this certainty is necessary before all else, in order to restore the Eucharist and priesthood to their absolutely central position, to have a proper sense of the importance of Holy Mass and Holy Communion, to return to eucharistic pedagogy, this being the source of priestly and religious vocations and inner strength for practising the Christian virtues ...

Today is a time for reflection, for meditation and for prayer for Christians to recover their sense of worship, their fervour. Only from the Eucharist profoundly known, loved and lived can we hope for that unity in truth and charity which is willed by Christ and urged on all by the Second Vatican Council.[6]

The Eucharist ... is the sacrament of his Body and Blood, which he himself has offered once and for all (cf. Hebrews 9:26–28), to set us free from sin and death, and which he has entrusted to his Church for her to make the same offering under the species of bread and wine and so to feed his faithful people for ever – that is, us who stand about his altar. The Eucharist is thus the sacrifice *par excellence*, that of Christ on the Cross, by means of which we receive Christ himself, Christ entire, God and man ...

The Son's sacrifice is unique and unrepeatable. It was made one single time in human history. And this unique and unrepeatable sacrifice 'endures'. The happening on Golgotha belongs to the past. The reality of the Trinity constitutes a divine 'today' for ever. Thus it is that all humanity shares in this 'today' of the Son's sacrifice. The Eucharist is the sacrament of this unfathomable 'today'. The Eucharist is the sacrament – the greatest one the Church has – by which the divine 'today' of the Redemption of the world meets our human 'today' in a manner ever human.'

We must once again emphasize how important it is, in obedience to the precept of the Church, to take part in the celebration of the Sunday Eucharist. For everyone, this is the highest act of worship in the exercise of the universal priesthood, just as the sacramental offering of the Mass is the highest act of worship, for priests, in the exercise of the priestly ministry. Participation in the eucharistic banquet is a vital condition for everyone for union with Christ, as he himself has said: 'In all truth I tell you, if you do not eat the flesh of the Son of man and drink his blood, you will have no life in you' (John 6:53). *The Catechism of the Catholic Church* reminds all the faithful about the significance of participating in the Sunday Eucharist (cf. nn. 2181–2182). Here I wish to conclude with those famous words in the First Letter of Peter, which portray the laity participating in the Eucharist-Church mystery: 'You too must become living stones making a spiritual house as a holy priesthood, to offer the spiritual sacrifices made acceptable to God through Jesus Christ' (1 Peter 2:5).[8]

For every faithful Catholic, participation at Holy Mass on Sunday is at once a duty and a privilege: a sweet obligation to respond to God's love for us, so that we can then bear witness to this love in our daily lives ... The fulfilling of the dominical precept ought, for every Christian family, to be a fundamental source of joy and unity. Every Sunday, all and every one of you have an appointment with God's love. Don't fail to keep it ...[9]

The Sacraments and Christian prayer

Instituted by the Saviour, Baptism is the first of the Sacraments; it abolishes 'original sin' and restores 'sanctifying grace' to the soul, introducing those who receive it into the trinitarian life of God and making them 'adoptive children' of the Father, brothers and sisters of Jesus, full members of the Christian Church – the Mystical Body of Christ – and heirs to the eternal joys of Paradise. To be born means entering into a specific divine plan: no one comes into the world by accident; on the contrary, everyone has a particular mission to perform, which, of course, we cannot know all about from the start but which will be made completely clear to us one day. So let us be guided by our awareness of being the instruments of a God who has created us out of love and wishes to be repaid with love by us.[10]

The Sacrament of Confirmation is, as it were, a completing of Baptism, the stage of maturity on the journey to full admittance into the mystery of Christ and to responsible acceptance of one's vocation in the Church. To understand the meaning of this sacrament, we need first of all to reflect on the function of all the Sacraments. They make the Gospel live again in us – that is to say, by them the figure, the life, the mysteries, the word, the events of Jesus' life are brought into our own lives and become part of our own being. Jesus draws near, enters our personal story through these physical and visible sacramental signs. With these signs Jesus calls us, associates us with his mission, makes us share in all the mysteries of his life. The event of Pentecost is essential to Jesus' mission, since the gift of the Holy Spirit enables Christ's disciples to grasp the whole truth about the Lord, and their spirits are reborn in their full participation in his supernatural life.[11]

The Anointing of the Sick does not prevent physical death; even less does it promise a miraculous curing of the human body. But it does always bring a special grace and comfort to the dying by preparing them to meet our loving Saviour with lively faith and love and in the firm hope of eternal life. Furthermore, it brings comfort and strength to those who are not about to die but who are suffering owing to serious illness or advanced age. For these, the Church pleads for healing, be it of body or soul, praying that the whole person may be renewed by the power of the Holy Spirit.

Whenever the Church celebrates this sacrament, she proclaims her belief in the victory of the Cross. It is as though we were repeating the words of St Paul: 'For I am certain of this: neither death nor life, nor angels, nor principalities, nothing already in existence and nothing still to come, nor any power, nor the heights nor the depths, nor any created thing whatever, will be able to come between us and the love of God, known to us in Christ Jesus our Lord' (Romans 8:38–39).[12]

Mary's motherly intercession

'Assist your people who have fallen yet strive to rise again!'

These words apply to every individual, every community, to nations and peoples, and to the generations and epochs of human history, to our own epoch, to these years of the Millennium which is drawing to a close; 'Assist, yes, assist your people who have fallen'!

This is the invocation addressed to Mary, the 'loving Mother of the Redeemer', the invocation addressed to Christ, who through Mary entered human history. Year after year the antiphon rises to Mary, evoking that moment which saw the accomplishment of this essential historical transformation from 'falling' to 'rising'.

Mankind has made wonderful discoveries and achieved extraordinary results in the fields of science and technology. It has made great advances along the path of progress and civilization, and in recent times one could say that it has succeeded in speeding up the pace of history. But the fundamental transformation, the one which can be called 'original', constantly accompanies man's journey, and through all the events of history accompanies each and every individual. It is the transformation from 'falling' to 'rising', from death to life. It is also *a constant challenge* to people's consciences, a challenge to man's whole historical awareness: the challenge to follow the path of 'not falling' in ways that are ever old and ever new, and of 'rising again' if a fall has occurred.[13]

The importance which the divine plan attaches to the person and mission of women is fully revealed in Mary. To convince ourselves of this, we have only to reflect on the anthropological importance of the fundamental aspects of Mariology: Mary is 'full of grace' from the first moment of her existence, so she is preserved from sin. Manifestly, God's favour is granted in abundance to this 'most blessed of women', and is reflected from Mary onto the very condition of womanhood, precluding any inferiority in it (cf. *Redemptoris Mater* 7–11).

Furthermore, Mary is involved in God's final covenant with the human race. She has the task of consenting, on behalf of mankind, to the coming of the Saviour. This role goes way beyond all the most recent demands for women's rights. Mary intervened in an outstanding and, humanly speaking, incredible way in human history, and by her consent contributed to the total transformation of human destiny.

Again: Mary co-operated in developing the mission of Jesus, be it by bringing him into the world, rearing him, standing beside him during the years of his hidden life; be it later, during the years of his public ministry, by discreetly supporting his activities, beginning at Cana, where she obtained the first manifestation of the Saviour's miraculous power. As the Council says, it was Mary who 'brought about by her intercession the beginning of the miracles of Jesus the Messiah' (*Lumen gentium* 58).

Above all, Mary co-operated with Christ in his redemptive work, not only by preparing Jesus for his mission but by uniting herself to his sacrifice for the salvation of all (cf. *Mulieris dignitatem* 3–5).

Today too, Mary's radiance can spread over the world of women, embracing old and new problems of womanhood, helping everyone to grasp its dignity and recognize its rights.[14]

The Rosary is my favourite prayer. A marvellous prayer. Marvellous in its simplicity and in its profundity. In this prayer we constantly repeat the words which the Virgin Mary heard from the Archangel and from her kinswoman Elizabeth.

The entire Church associates herself with these words. In a certain way, one might say, the Rosary is a commentary-prayer on the final chapter of the Constitution *Lumen gentium* of Vatican II, the chapter treating of the wonderful presence of the Mother of God in the mystery of Christ and his Church. For, against the background of the words '*Ave Maria*', the principal episodes of Christ's life pass before the eyes of the soul. They consist of the sum of joyful, sorrowful and glorious mysteries, and put us in living fellowship with Jesus through – we can say – his Mother's heart. At the same time, in these decades of the Rosary, our hearts can contain all the events making up the life of the individual, of the family, of the nation, of the Church, of the human race; things that happen to us, to our neighbour and particularly to those who are nearest to us, those whom we hold dearest. So the simple prayer of the Rosary keeps time with the rhythm of human life.[15]

Popular devotions, popular piety

I have in mind devotions practised by the faithful in certain regions with moving fervour and purity of intention, even if the faith underlying them needs to be purified or rectified in many aspects. I have in mind certain easily understood prayers that many simple people are fond of repeating. I have in mind certain acts of piety practised with a sincere desire to do penance or to please the Lord. Underlying most of these prayers and practices, besides elements that should be discarded, there are other elements which, if they were properly used, could serve very well to help people advance towards knowledge of the mystery of Christ and of his message: the love and mercy of God, the Incarnation of Christ, his redeeming Cross and Resurrection, the activity of the Spirit in each Christian and in the Church, the mystery of the hereafter, the evangelical virtues to be practised, the presence of the Christian in the world, and so on ... And why should we appeal to non-Christian or even anti-Christian elements, refusing to build on elements which, even if they need to be revised and improved, have something Christian at their root?[16]

Popular piety is a true treasure of the People of God. It is a continual demonstration of the active presence of the Holy Spirit in the Church. He it is who kindles faith, hope and love in hearts, the lofty virtues that give meaning to Christian piety. It is the same Spirit who ennobles the various ways in which the Christian message is expressed, to harmonize with the culture and manners pertaining to every place and in every age.

All genuinely Christian popular devotions must be faithful to Christ's message and the Church's teachings. Popular piety should always lead on to liturgical piety, and that means conscious and active participation in the common prayer of the Church. These Church services, towards which popular religious observances should meekly converge, are unquestionably moments of grace. The feasts of the patron saints of each place, times of mission, pilgrimages to shrines, are so many invitations which the Lord addresses to the whole community – and to each individual – to follow in the way of salvation.

But don't wait for these great holidays to come round. Go to Sunday Mass, thus sanctifying the Lord's Day by devoting it to divine worship, to lawful rest and a more intense family life. Act in such a way that no day will go by without moments of personal or family prayer within the home-church – that is, the family – so that your whole existence may be flooded by the light and grace of God.[17]

Spiritual childhood, the secret of salvation

St Matthew the Evangelist tells how 'Jesus called a little child to him whom he set among them. Then he said, "In truth I tell you, unless you change and become like little children you will never enter the kingdom of Heaven. And so, the one who makes himself as little as this little child is the greatest in the kingdom of Heaven"' (Matthew 18:2–4).

This is Jesus' disturbing response: to enter the Kingdom of Heaven, it is absolutely essential to become little and humble, like children. Clearly

Jesus doesn't want to make Christians stay in a state of perpetual childishness, or self-satisfied ignorance, of indifference to the problems of the times. Quite the reverse! Yet he holds the child up as the model for entering the Kingdom of Heaven, because of the symbolism inherent in childhood:

First of all, the child is innocent, and the first requisite for entering the Kingdom of Heaven is the life of 'grace' – that is to say, of innocence preserved or reacquired, the exclusion of sin which is always an act of pride and selfishness.

Secondly, the child lives by faith, trusting in its parents, and surrenders itself entirely to those who guide and love it. Christians too must be humble and must surrender themselves in perfect trust to Christ and the Church. The great danger, the great enemy, is always pride, and Jesus insists on the virtue of humility, since one cannot but be humble before the Infinite. Humility is truth; it is also a sign of intelligence and the source of serenity.

Lastly, the child is content with little things, and these suffice to make it happy: a small success, a good mark deserved, praise received, will send it wild with joy.

To enter the Kingdom of Heaven, we have to have great, immense, universal aspirations; but we need to know how to be satisfied with little things, with the tasks imposed by obedience, with God's will as expressed in the fleeting moment, with the daily joys offered by Providence. Of every piece of work, however hidden and modest, we need to make a masterpiece of love and perfection.

We have to be converted to littleness in order to enter the Kingdom of Heaven. We recall St Thérèse of Lisieux's brilliant intuition when meditating on the verse in Holy Scripture: 'Who is little, let him come to me' (Proverbs 9:4). She realized that the sense of 'littleness' was like a lift which could more swiftly and more easily carry her to the peak of holiness: 'Your arms, O Jesus, are the lift that must raise me to heaven! This is why I have absolutely no need to become great; rather, I need to stay little and to become smaller still.'[18]

IV

LOVE

The path of goodness has a name:
it is called love;
in it we can find the key to every hope,
for true love has its root
in God himself.

*Creating man and woman 'in his own image and
likeness', God intended them to be collaborators
with him in the creative plan – that is to say, first of
all in giving life to new creatures and then in improving life by means of work, science, art, medicine, and
hence too in redeeming and exalting life, given the
inclination to evil in human nature.*

*Given God's omnipotence, he could always have
created each man and woman individually, as he did
our First Parents; but instead he chose to create by
means of man and woman, formed for the very purpose of collaborating with him in giving life; whence
is born the mutual love of man and woman in order
to give life to a new creature, the fruit of the love of*

God, who creates the souls and love of its parents.
The sexual intimacy between man and woman thus
becomes sacred and is founded on monogamous,
faithful marriage and on the Sacrament conferring a
special divine grace, of which husband and wife are
themselves the ministers.

God is love

The greatest proof of God's love is that he loves us in
our human condition, with our weaknesses and needs.
Nothing else can explain the mystery of the Cross.

Christ's love is more powerful than sin and death.
St Paul explains that Christ came to forgive sins
and that his love is greater than any sin whatever,
greater than my sins and those of anyone else. This is
the Church's faith. This is the Good News of God's
love, which the Church has proclaimed down the
ages and which I proclaim to you today: God loves
you with an everlasting love. He loves you in Christ
Jesus his Son.

God's love shows itself in various ways. In particular, God loves us as our Father. The parable of the
Prodigal Son expresses this truth very clearly. You
remember the moment in the parable when the son
comes to his senses and decides to go home? He sets
off for his father's house. 'While he was still a long
way off, his father saw him and was moved with pity.
He ran to the boy, clasped him in his arms and kissed
him' (Luke 15:20). This is God's fatherly love, a love

ever ready to forgive, anxious to welcome us home.

God's love for us as our Father is a strong and faithful love, a love full of compassion, a love that allows us to hope for the grace of conversion, when we have sinned.

God loves all of you, boundlessly, without distinction. He loves the oldest of you who feel the weight of your years. He loves the sick and those suffering from AIDS and the problems linked to this. He loves the relatives and friends of the sick, those who look after them. He loves us all with an unconditional, everlasting love.

Cast away your doubts and fears and let God's compassion draw you to his heart. Open the doors of your heart to our God; he is rich in mercy. 'What great love the Father has lavished on us by letting us be called God's children – which is what we are!' (1 John 3:1). Yes, we are this today and always: children of a loving God!¹

God alone is good, which means that in him and only in him all values have their earliest origin and ultimate fulfilment; he is 'Alpha and Omega, the beginning and the end'. Only in him are their authenticity and final confirmation to be found. Without him – without reference to God – the whole world of created values stays as though suspended in an absolute void. It loses its transparency, its power of expression too. Evil appears as good; good is discredited. Doesn't experience itself in our own day show this to be so, wherever God has been banished beyond the horizon of appraisals, of evaluations, of actions?

Why is only God good? *Because he is love.* Christ gives this answer in the Gospel words and, above all, in the witness of his own life and death: 'for God so loved the world that he gave his only-begotten Son.' God is good precisely because 'he is love'.[2]

Love

The path of goodness has a name: it is called love. In it we can find the key to every hope, for true love has its root in God himself. 'We have recognised for ourselves, and put our faith in, the love God has for us. God is love (1 John 4:16).

Love is the constructive force for humanity's every positive road. The future does not gather hopes from violence, from hatred, from the intrusiveness of individual or collective selfishness. Deprived of love, we fall victim to an insidious spiral for ever contracting the horizons of brotherhood while prompting each of us to make ourselves, our own ego and our own pleasure, the only criterion of judgement. The egocentric point of view, the cause of the impoverishment of true love, gives rise to the worst snares present today in the world of the young.

Lack of love means yielding to indifference and scepticism; lack of love means becoming enslaved to drugs and a disordered sexuality; lack of love means surrendering ourselves to organizations based on violence and operating by illegal and high-handed means.[3]

Without genuine mutual love the family cannot live, cannot thrive, cannot develop as a community of persons; such love as this brings the living gift of children, and builds up mutual loyalty and fellowship with other families. All this demands a great spirit of sacrifice and a generous willingness to understand, to forgive, to be reconciled, so preventing selfishness, discord and tensions from striking root within the family circle.

Loving is essentially a giving of oneself to others. Far from being an instinctive inclination, love is a conscious decision of the will to go out to others. To be able to love properly, one must detach oneself from many things and above all from self; one must give freely, one must love to the end. This stripping away of self – a long job – is laborious and exciting. It is the source of equilibrium. It is the secret of happiness.[4]

Respect for the body

However material the body may be, it is not an object like any other object. First of all, it is someone, in the sense that it is a manifestation of the person, a means of being present to other people, of communicating with them, of all sorts of expression. The body is a word, a language. What a marvel, and at the same time what a danger! Young men, boys – have great respect for your own bodies and for those of others! Let your body be at the service of your inner self! Let your gestures, your looks, be ever the reflection of your soul! Worship of the body? No, never! Contempt for the body? Even less! Control of the body! Yes! Transfiguration of the body! Even more so![5]

Do not let yourselves be carried away by sexual excitement, for this puts genuine human love at risk and leads to the break-up of the family. St Paul writes, 'Do you not know that your body is the temple of the Holy Spirit, who is in you?' (1 Corinthians 3:16).

Girls, you must strive after true feminism, the authentic realization of the woman as a human person, as an integral part of the family and society, consciously playing your part in accordance with your true qualities.[6]

We are the children of an age when, owing to the development of various disciplines, this integral vision of human nature can easily be rejected and replaced by any number of partial concepts; these, by dwelling on one or other aspect of the *compositum humanum*, either do not embrace the human *integrum* or leave it completely out of account. Various cultural tendencies then come into play which – on the basis of these partial truths – formulate their own theories and practical proposals with regard to human behaviour and, even more often, on how to behave towards humanity. The human being then becomes the object of determinate techniques, rather than a subject responsible for his or her own actions.

That theology also includes the body should not surprise anyone who is aware of the mystery and reality of the Incarnation. By virtue of the fact that the Word of God became flesh, the body – one might say – has entered theology through the main gate, theology being the science that has the divine as its object of study. The Incarnation – and the Redemption springing from it – has likewise become the definitive source of the sacramental nature of marriage.

Contemporary biophysics can furnish much precise information on human sexuality. Knowledge about the dignity of the human body and sex, however, is to be obtained at other fountains – particularly from the very word of God, which contains revelation concerning the body, going back to the beginning of the world.

How significant it is that Christ, in answer to all these questions, bids us return, in a sense, to the threshold of our theological history! He bids us put ourselves on the boundary between original innocence-happiness and the heritage of the first fall. Does he not perhaps want to say, in this way, that the way by which he leads humankind, male-female, in the Sacrament of Marriage – that is, the way of the 'redemption of the body' – should consist in the recovery of this dignity in which the true significance of the human body is achieved: its significance simultaneously as individual and 'in fellowship'?'

Sexuality in God's plan

Sexuality belongs to the original plan of the Creator, and the Church cannot but hold it in high esteem. Neither at the same time can she refrain from asking each of us to respect it in its deeper nature.

As a dimension inscribed in the totality of the person, sexuality is a specific 'language' in the service of love, and must not therefore be lived as mere instinctuality. It must be controlled by us as intelligent, free beings.

This is not, however, to say that it can be manipulated arbitrarily. For it possesses its own typical psychological and biological structure, directed either to fellowship between man and woman, or to the birth of new persons. To respect this structure and this indissoluble connection is not 'biologism' or 'moralism'; it is concern for the truth about human beings, about being a person. It is by virtue of this truth, which is even evident to the light of reason, that so-called 'free love', homosexuality and contraception are morally unacceptable. For these are types of behaviour which distort the deep significance of human sexuality, by preventing it from being at the service of the person, of fellowship and of new life.

The Church is sometimes accused of making a 'taboo' out of sex. The truth is quite the opposite. In the course of history, in contrast to Manichaean trends, Christian thought has developed a harmonious and positive view of human nature, by recognizing the significant and valuable role that masculine and feminine play in human life.

The biblical message is unequivocal: 'God created man in his own image ... Male and female created he them' (Genesis 1:27). Into this statement is sculpted the dignity of every man and every woman, in their equality of nature, yet in their diversity as well.

It is a *datum* deeply affecting the constitution of the human being, 'for from its sex, the human person derives the characteristics which on the biological, psychological and spiritual planes make it man or woman' (*Persona humana* 1).

I stressed this in my *Letter to Families*. This is what I said: 'Human beings were created "from the beginning" as male and female; the life of all humanity – of small communities as of society as a whole – is marked by this primordial duality. From it there derive the "masculinity" and the "femininity" of individuals, just as from it every community draws its own unique richness in the mutual fulfilment of persons' (n. 6)[8]

Continence for the Kingdom of Heaven

Although continence 'for the sake of the Kingdom of Heaven' undoubtedly means a renunciation, this *renunciation* is also an *affirmation*: one that comes from the discovery of the 'gift' – that is, from discovering a new view of personal self-realization 'by means of a sincere giving of oneself' (*Gaudium et Spes* 24). This discovery, then, is in deep inner harmony with the sense of the marital significance of the body, linked 'from the beginning' to the masculinity or femininity of the human being as a personal subject. Although continence 'for the Kingdom of Heaven' is identified with renunciation of marriage – which in the lives of man and woman gives rise to the family – one may in no way see it as a denial of the essential value of marriage. On the contrary, indeed, continence serves indirectly to throw into relief what in the conjugal vocation is perennial and most profoundly personal, that which in the dimensions of temporality (and also in the perspective of the 'world to come') corresponds to the dignity of the personal gift, linked to the conjugal significance of the body in its masculinity or femininity.[9]

The significance and value of marriage

Marriage is orientated towards duration, towards the future. It looks beyond its own confines. Marriage is the only place which is fit for the begetting and bringing-up of children. So married love is also in essence orientated towards fertility. In this task of handing on life, husband and wife collaborate with God the Creator's love. I know that even here, in today's society, there are big difficulties. Increasingly so, especially for women. Housing shortages, economic and medical problems, and indeed, often an attitude which is overtly unfavourable to large families, are obstacles to greater fertility. I appeal to all those in positions of responsibility, to all social forces: do all you can to help. I appeal first of all to your consciences, to your sense of personal responsibility, dear brothers and sisters. In your conscience, before God, you should decide how many children you would like.

As husbands and wives you are called to responsible parenthood. But this means the kind of family planning that respects the ethical norms and criteria.[10]

Entering on the way of the vocation of marriage means *learning marital love* day by day, year by year: love according to soul and body, the love that 'is patient and kind, that never seeks its own advantage and does not take offence'; the love that 'finds its joy in the truth', the love that 'endures whatever comes' (1 Corinthians 13:4–7).

This is exactly the love you need, young people, if your future marriages are to stand the test of a lifetime. And this test is itself part of the very essence of the vocation which, by means of marriage, you intend to inscribe in your plan of life.

Today the principles of Christian matrimonial morality are presented distortedly in many circles. In some, there is an attempt to impose – indeed, this applies to entire societies – a model which is self-proclaimed as 'progressive' and 'modern'. People do not realize at the time that in this model men and, perhaps even more so, women are changed from subjects into objects (objects specifically to be manipulated), and all of love's great content is reduced to 'enjoyment' which, even were it to involve both parties, would not cease to be basically selfish. Lastly, the child, the fruit and new embodiment of the couple's love, becomes a more and more 'tiresome adjunct'. The materialistic, consumerist civilization penetrates this marvellous whole of conjugal, fatherly and motherly love, robbing it of that deeply humane content, which since the beginning of the world has been pervaded by a mark and reflection of the divine.[11]

The tragedy of divorce
and the motherhood of the Church

The Church knows she is 'swimming against the stream' when she proclaims the principle of the indissolubility of the marriage bond. The service which she owes to humanity obliges her constantly to drive home this truth, appealing to the voice of conscience which, even amid the weightiest conditioning, is never entirely silenced in the human breast.

I am well aware that this aspect of matrimonial ethics is one of the most *demanding*. And sometimes really difficult matrimonial situations occur, if not actually tragic ones. For these situations, the Church seeks to show understanding, like Jesus in his compassion. Jesus explains how even in the Old Testament the value of indissolubility had become so obscured that divorce came to be tolerated. He explained that the concession of the Mosaic law was due to 'the hardness of the human heart', and he did not hesitate to reimpose God's original plan in all its vigour, as set out in the book of Genesis: 'The man will leave his father and mother and cleave to his wife, and they will become *one flesh*' (Genesis 2:24), and adding: 'Whom God has joined together, let no man put asunder' (Matthew 19:6).

Someone might object that this line of teaching is only intelligible and valid within a religious context. Not so! True, for Christ's disciples, indissolubility is further reinforced by the 'sacramental' character of marriage, a sign of the marriage-alliance between Christ and his Church. But this 'great mystery' (cf. Ephesians 5:32) does not exclude – indeed, it even presupposes – the ethical instance of indissolubility even on the level of natural law. It is, alas, that hard-heartedness condemned by Jesus which still makes it difficult for everyone to perceive this truth, or to determine cases in which it would seem virtually impossible to live. When, however, we reason calmly, keeping the ideal before us, it is not difficult to agree that the permanency of the marriage bond arises from the very essence of love and of the family. We only love really and truly when we love *for ever*, in sorrow and in joy, in good times and bad. Don't the children too have an absolute need of the indissoluble union of their parents? Aren't they, as often as not, the first victims of the tragedy of divorce?[12]

Faced with the difficulties that can arise in married life, do not let yourselves be thrown off course by the easy expedient of divorce, for this offers only apparent solutions: in actual fact its only effect is to transfer the problems into other spheres and make them worse. Christians know that marriage, being by its nature indissoluble, has been sanctioned by Christ, who has made it share in the faithful, indestructible love between himself and the Church (cf. Ephesians 5:32). Faced with the tensions and conflicts that can arise, especially when the family is enclosed in an atmosphere impregnated with permissiveness and hedonism, let its members remember that 'the God of peace is constantly calling them to undergo the joyful and renewing experience of reconciliation, that is, of fellowship re-established, of unity restored' (*Familiaris consortio* 21). In a special way, by sharing in the sacrament of reconciliation and in the communion of the Body of Christ, Christian families will find the strength and grace necessary for the over-coming of obstacles that threaten their unity, not for-getting, what is more, that true love is purified by suffering.[13]

Today there are many more cases of people who are on their own, to whom the Church cannot be indif-ferent but must show care. First, there is the category of the 'separated' and the 'divorced', to whom I have paid particular attention in the Apostolic Exhortation *Familiaris consortio* (cf. n. 83). Then there is that of 'unmarried mothers', who are exposed to particular difficulties of the moral, economic and social order. To all these people I want to say that, whatever their personal responsibility may be in the tragedy in which they find themselves involved, *they still belong to the Church*. Sharing in their trials, the pas-tors will not forsake them, but rather will do the best they can to help them, comfort them and make them still feel part of Christ's fold.

Even when unable to countenance practices which would conflict with the demands of truth and with the general good of families and societies, the Church never gives up loving, understanding and being close to those who are in trouble. The Church feels a particular sympathy for those who, having a broken marriage behind them, loyally persevere and, forgo-ing a second marriage, devote themselves, as best they may, to bringing up their children. They deserve everyone's support and encouragement. The Church, the Pope, cannot praise them enough for their fine and consistent witness to Christian values, generous-heartedly lived in testing circumstances.[14]

The moral relativism of modern society

Modern society's temptation is relativism, which turns many people into sceptics. Cultural changes and scientific progress in particular seem to disturb the criteria of discernment in matters of morality. Objective moral values and reference-points are hardly acknowledged. Individualism and subjectivism become the dominant factors in ethical thought and decision-making. It could be said that at times certain types of behaviour come to be regarded as normal and morally acceptable because they are common to vast numbers of people. Confusion reigns once we allow ourselves to believe that whatever is legal is of its nature moral, especially where civil laws are contrary to the demands of morality. Many of our contemporaries, as yet not open to the hope of Christian salvation and a sense of sin, have new kinds of anxiety to endure, and this can cast a blight over their whole lives.

The purpose of medicine and medical research is to serve life, to make it possible for people to live every phase of their existence in the dignity and humanity proper to them. Society and the civil authorities have a duty to protect people, particularly the frailest ones, from the possible excesses of science and technology.

Many questions arise in connection with scientific and therapeutic choices. Decisions, however, should not be made without taking account of the nature of every human being – a nature which is worthy of infinite respect. The human being is a creature loved by God, with an inalienable right to live and to be protected, from its very conception till its natural death. To refuse life to the weakest and the handicapped is a real outrage to all those who, for various reasons, live in such circumstances. This constitutes an unavowed form of eugenics. Furthermore, whatever the prognosis may be, radical therapeutic choices can never be justified when based on an arbitrary and subjective definition of the quality of life and of solely medical and scientific criteria.[15]

The family

The family is the domestic Church. The meaning of this traditional Christian idea is that the home is the Church in miniature.

The Church is the Sacrament of God's love. She is a fellowship of faith and life. She is mother and teacher. She is at the service of the whole human family on the journey to its final destination.

The family too is a fellowship of life and love. It trains and guides its members towards full human maturity and serves for the good of all along life's road. The family is the 'vital primary cell of society'

(*Apostolicam Actuositatem* 11). The future of the world and the Church thus pass through the family.

Genuine love is always responsible love. Husbands and wives truly love one another when they act responsibly before God and carry out his plan for human love and human life; when they respond and are responsible one for the other. Responsible fatherhood implies not only bringing babies into the world but taking a personal and responsible part in their growth and upbringing. In the family, true love is for ever.[16]

Contemporary society particularly needs the witness of couples who persevere in their marriage, as an eloquent 'sign' (even though at times it may be hard to bear), in our human condition, of the constancy of God's love. Day by day Christian married couples are called to open their hearts ever wider to the Holy Spirit, whose power will never fail, and who will enable them to love one another as Christ has loved us. From this love Christian families are born. In them, children are welcomed as a splendid gift bestowed by God's goodness of heart, and brought up in the fundamental values of human life, above all by learning that 'it is what a man is, rather than what he has, that counts' (*Gaudium et Spes* 35). The whole family seeks to practise respect for the dignity of each individual and to offer a disinterested service to those most in need of it (cf. *Familiaris consortio* 37).[17]

The procreative responsibility of parents

The Catechism of the Catholic Church points out that conjugal love 'naturally tends to be fruitful. A child does not come from outside as something added on to the mutual love of the spouses, but springs from the very heart of their mutual giving as its fruit and fulfilment' (CCC 2366).

It is fundamentally important to grasp the mysterious greatness of this event. As I wrote in my *Letter to Families*, 'in human fatherhood and motherhood ... *God himself is present* ... For God alone is the source of that *image and likeness* which is proper to the human being, as it was received at the creation. Procreation is the continuation of the creation' (n. 9).

Of course, this address has a particular resonance for believers. But its importance is also obvious for the simple reason that, in the miracle of the birth of human life, we are obliged to recognize something going far beyond a mere biological fact. In the procreation of human life, *biology postulates its own transcendence.* And that cannot but have implications on the ethical plane too: we cannot treat that which obtains in the procreation of human life as though we were dealing with a mere biological event, susceptible of various kinds of manipulation.

It is on this fundamental anthropological and ethical basis that the Church's doctrine of 'responsible fatherhood and motherhood' rests. Alas, on this point Catholic thought is often misunderstood, as though the Church supported an ideology of fecundity to the last by urging married couples to procreate without common sense or planning. But careful reading of the pronouncements of the magisterium is enough to show that this is not so.

Actually, in the procreation of life, husband and wife realize one of the highest dimensions of their vocation: *they are collaborating with God*. Because this is so, they are bound to take an extremely responsible attitude. In taking the decision to have or not to have a child, they must let themselves be inspired, not by selfishness or thoughtlessness, but by a prudent and informed generosity which weighs up the possibilities and circumstances and, above all, makes the well-being of the future child its central consideration. When, therefore, there is good reason for not procreating, this choice is lawful and may even be a duty. But there is also a duty to do this by criteria and methods that respect the total truth of the conjugal encounter in its unitive and procreative dimension, which is wisely regulated by nature itself in its biological rhythms. These may be complied with and put to advantage but not 'violated' by artificial interference.[18]

Unfortunately, even in the delicate sphere of the procreation of life, there are worrying symptoms of a culture very different from that inspired by true love. This is all too clear when unborn life is excluded or even suppressed; but, paradoxically, this also applies in the case where a child is 'wanted', cost what it may, and when morally disordered means are used to this end. For techniques of human procreation which cause serious ethical problems – such as artificial insemination, surrogate motherhood and the like – are spreading faster and faster. Among other grave implications, suffice it to note that, in such procedures, human beings are defrauded of the right to be born from a true act of love and by normal biological processes, thus being marked from the outset by problems of a psychological, legal and social order, which will remain with them throughout their lives.

In fact, the legitimate desire for a child cannot be interpreted as a sort of *right to a child*, to be satisfied *at any cost*. That would be to treat the child on the level of a thing! As for science, its duty is to maintain the natural generative processes, not to replace them by artificial means. All the more so since the desire for children can also be satisfied through the legal institution of adoption, which deserves to be ever better organized and promoted, and other forms of social service and dedication, such as fostering children, all too many of whom, for various reasons, are deprived of the warmth of a family.[19]

Woman's vocation to motherhood

Today, perhaps as never before, it is necessary to reassess the idea of motherhood. This is no archaic

concept belonging to the mythological beginnings of
civilization. However much new roles may open up
for women, everything in women – their physiology,
their psychology, their more or less innate behaviour,
their moral, religious and even aesthetic sense –
reveals and enhances their disposition, capacity and
mission to bring new life into the world. They, much
more than men, are involved in the generative
process. By virtue of pregnancy and childbirth, they
are more closely linked to the child, more involved in
its entire development, more immediately responsible for its growth, with a more intense share in the
joys, sorrows and dangers of its life. Though it is true
that a mother's task must be co-ordinated with the
presence and responsibility of the father, the woman
is the one who plays the more important role at the
start of every human life. It is a role in which an
essential characteristic of the human person is made
plain: people are destined not to stay shut in on
themselves, but to open up and give themselves to
others.[20]

The role of the mother must be socially reassessed.
The mother's tasks in the home demand great commitment, much time and much love. Children need
looking after, they need love and affection. Care has
to be taken if the children are to become secure and
responsible adults – that is, morally, religiously and
psychologically mature. If responsibility for the

development of the family belongs rather to the mother than to the father, even more depends on the particular relationship between mother and child.

A society can indeed be proud of itself if it allows mothers to devote time to their children, and if it allows them to bring them up in accordance with their needs. Women's freedom as mothers should be clearly protected, so that they are free from all discrimination, especially in relation to women with no family obligations. Mothers must not be financially penalized by the very society that they so usefully and nobly serve.[21]

By motherhood, God has entrusted human beings to women in an entirely special way. This is why the leading role in protecting life from the moment of its conception pertains to women. Who more than a mother can know the miracle of a life unfolding in her womb?

Women, alas, often encounter objective difficulties, making their maternal task more onerous for them, sometimes to the point of heroism.

We must energetically repulse all the many forms of violence and exploitation which, more or less overtly, capitalize on women and trample on their dignity.

Not seldom, these unbearable pressures derive from indifference and inadequate help. They are due too to legal systems which are poorly attuned to the importance of the family. They are also caused by a widespread and distorted culture which unduly excuses a man from his family responsibilities and, in the worst cases, encourages him to regard women as objects of pleasure or mere instruments of reproduction.

Against this oppressive culture, every legitimate initiative must be taken, with a view to promoting the genuine emancipation of women. But in this task, the dignity of womanhood and the protection of life go hand in hand.[22]

Feminism: exaggerations and provocations

In some circles there is still a feeling of dissatisfaction over the Church's position, particularly where there is a lack of clear understanding of the distinction between a person's human and civil rights, and the rights, duties, ministries and functions which individuals have or by which they benefit within the Church. A mistaken ecclesiology can easily lead to presenting false needs and raising false hopes.

What is certain is that the question cannot be resolved by compromising with a feminism which is polarized on ideologically intransigent positions. It is not merely a matter of some people claiming the right for women to be admitted to the ordained priesthood. Where this issue is carried to extremes, the Christian religion itself is in danger of being undermined. Sometimes forms of nature worship and the celebration of myths and symbols take the place of the worship of God revealed in Jesus Christ. Unfortunately, this type of feminism is encouraged by some people within the Church, including some religious whose opinions, attitudes and behaviour no longer correspond with what is taught by the Gospel and the Church. As pastors, we must oppose individuals and groups holding such opinions, and we must summon them to sincere and honest dialogue to be carried on within the Church on the topic of women's expectations.

Regarding non-admission of women to the ministerial priesthood, this 'is a practice that the Church has always found in the expressed will of Christ, totally free and sovereign' (*Christifideles laici* 51). The Church teaches and works trusting in the presence of the Holy Spirit and in the Lord's promise to be always with her (Matthew 28:18–20). 'When she considers that she cannot accept certain changes, it is because she knows that she is bound to act as Christ acts. Her attitude ... is that of fidelity' (*Inter insigniores* 4). The equality of the baptized – one of the great affirmations of Christianity – exists in a differentiated body, in which men and women have roles which are not merely functional but are deeply rooted in Christian anthropology and in the Christian sacramental system. The distinction of roles in no way favours the superiority of one over the other: the best gift of all, which can and should be desired, is charity (cf. 1 Corinthians 12–13). In the Kingdom of God, the greatest are not the ministers, but the saints.[23]

The population explosion

The Church is aware of the problem and does not underestimate its significance. Precisely because this is so, she has recently promoted and encouraged deeper studies, taking account of the statistical data and appraising the ethical and pastoral implications. She acknowledges the responsibility of governments in this delicate sphere. In the *Catechism* it is expressly stated that the public authority may take measures 'to orient the demography of the population' (CCC 2372).

Such measures obviously presuppose a responsible attitude in families themselves. As I have already had occasion to say, married couples should decide to have their children in accordance with a reasonable plan, based on a generous but at the same time realistic assessment of their potentialities, of the well-being of the future child and that of society itself, by the light of objective moral criteria (cf. Message to Mrs Nafis Sadik, *Observatore Romano*, 19 March 1994, p. 8).

In this field, family ethics and political ethics meet. The ethical dimension sets precise limits to the degree to which governments and the international community may intervene. For example, it is never lawful to intervene by 'authoritarian, coercive measures' (CCC 2372) to deprive married couples of their primary and inalienable responsibility. It is also unacceptable to encourage the use of immoral means, particularly those procuring abortion, for birth control. This is one of the points of radical disagreement between the Church and some tendencies now emerging. For indeed, how can one fail to be disturbed by the fact that certain agencies are prepared to spend huge sums of money in order to spread ethically inadmissable means of contraception, while refusing to develop the great potential of 'natural family planning'? For this, besides being less costly, is certainly 'helpful to couples in preserving their human dignity in the exercise of responsible love-making' (Appeal of the Cardinals in defence of the family, *Osservatore Romano*, 15 June 1994, p. 1).

It is clear that for a right solution to demographical politics there needs to be intensified commitment either to a growth of natural and economic resources, or to their more equitable distribution. There also needs to be proper international co-operation in developing less favoured countries.[24]

The protection of life from the first moment

The Council did not hesitate to describe abortion as an 'abominable crime' (*Gaudium et Spes* 51). The basis for such a severe judgement lies not only in the revealed word of God but also *in human reason*.

Science itself today bears its own witness to the human character of the embryo, by assuring us that from the moment of its conception it is an original and biologically autonomous being, endowed with an internal programme which will keep operating until it has developed to maturity. For this reason alone, God's commandment 'Thou shalt not kill' applies no less to the embryo than to people who have already been born.

The State has a duty to guarantee and foster respect for the life of every human being by every way possible. Against this duty one cannot invoke freedom of conscience or freedom of choice, since respect for life is the foundation of every other right, including those to do with freedom. As the *Catechism of the Catholic Church* states, 'the inalienable right of life of every innocent human individual is a constitutive element of a civil society and its legislation' (CCC 2273), and 'the moment a positive law deprives a category of human beings of that protection which civil legislation should accord them, the State denies the equality of all before the law. When the State does not use its strength to maintain the rights of every citizen and in particular of those who are weakest, the very foundations of a constitutional State are undermined' (Congregation for the Doctrine of the Faith, Instruction *Donum vitae* c.III).[25]

Bringing up children

Bringing up children to the great values of the Christian Faith: to faith in God the Father, in Christ his Son, in the Holy Spirit! The first school of religious instruction is and ought to be the family. From father, from mother, from brothers and sisters, as well as receiving examples of Christian living, most little children should also receive the treasure of the great truths of Divine Revelation. These will be better understood later with organized religious teaching in parishes, institutes and movements.

But above all, parents, you must train your children to pray; introduce them to the progressive discovery of the mystery of God and to personal dialogue with him. This praying done in the family – which is the domestic Church – is children's natural introduction to the liturgical prayer of the Church entire. So there must be a progressive participation by all members of the Christian family in the Eucharist, above all on Sundays and feast-days, and in the other sacraments, in particular those of Christian initiation.[26]

Children need parents who can give them a stable family environment: parents who understand what genuine love children need in order to feel that they are sharing in the parents' love for others and for them. To you they look for friendship and guidance. From you, above all, they must learn the difference between right and wrong and how to tell good from evil. I appeal to you: do not deprive your children of their true human and spiritual heritage. Talk to them about God, about Jesus, about his love and about his Gospel. Teach them to love God and to keep his commandments, in the sure certainty that they are, before all else, his children. Teach them to pray. Teach them to become mature, responsible human beings and upright citizens of their country.[27]

With the grace of Christian marriage, husband and wife can build their marital home together in trust and hope. They can bring their children into it, so that they may learn from their parents what it means to be men and women, and learn to live their human and Christian dignity to the full.

By its very nature, the family is called to be the child's first sphere of training. The duties of bringing up the child take priority, they override all else. The parents do the upbringing, and through them Christ himself brings the children up. In bringing up their children, parents in fact also educate themselves. They learn what responsible love is. In cultivating the soil of the young hearts of their children, they deepen the formation of their own hearts as well. This is why, today, the Church invokes the Holy Spirit with the words: '*Veni Creator Spiritus*', so that he, the author of all good and the source of all holiness, may visit your hearts and help you to form the home-Church as the fruit of the sacrament of marriage.[28]

V

HISTORY

It is important to explain
that the history of the human race,
marked as it is by grace and sin,
greatness and misery,
is taken up by God in his Son Jesus Christ,
foreshadowing in some way the age that is to come.

Understood not as a narrative of past events but as development of logically linked events, history has meaning and purpose.

With our reason we can easily discern that human history is in continuous development and progress: the cave-man with his tom-tom has slowly and laboriously arrived at the skyscraper, television, the computer, jet aircraft. Hence reason tells us that the purpose of history is human progress.

But the light of Revelation tells us once and for all what the real purpose of history is. Christian Revelation tells us that all human history is 'salvation history', progressing through three definite stages: Creation, Redemption and final Recompense.

Revelation teaches that God has willed and still wills human history, he having created men and women as intelligent, free beings; and with the Incarnation, he has himself entered human history to redeem it. Human beings collaborate with God in the perfecting, completing and redeeming of 'human nature' – that is to say, in the development and progress of history.

The meaning of history

What is the meaning of life? And what, in consequence, is the meaning of human history?

It is certainly the most dramatic of questions – and the noblest too – revealing human beings in their true nature, as persons endowed with intelligence and will. For we cannot shut ourselves within the confines of time, within the circle of matter, within the node of an immanent and self-sufficient existence. We may try to do so; we may even affirm by word and deed that our homeland is only time and our dwelling-place only the body. But in fact the supreme question keeps worrying us, stinging and tormenting us. It is a question that will not go away.

We are aware that, unfortunately, much of modern, atheistic, agnostic, secularized thought persistently states and teaches that the supreme question is in fact a human malady, a psychological and emotional exaggeration, from which we need to be cured by bravely facing up to the absurd, to death, to nothingness.

It is a subtly dangerous philosophy, above all because young people – still unsure in their convictions, shaken by the unhappy events of past and present history, by instability and uncertainty about the future, at times betrayed in their deepest affections, marginalized, misunderstood, unemployed – may feel driven by it to seek a way out through drugs and violence, or to give up hope.

Jesus Christ alone is the adequate and final answer to the supreme question about the meaning of life and history.[1]

It is important to explain that the history of the human race, marked as it is by grace and sin, greatness and misery, is taken up by God in his son Jesus Christ, 'foreshadowing in some way the age that is to come'.

Finally it is important frankly to reveal the demands – demands that involve self-denial but also joy – made by what the Apostle Paul liked to call 'newness of life', 'a new creation', 'being in Christ', and 'eternal life in Christ Jesus', which is the same thing as life in the world, but lived in accordance with the Beatitudes and with a calling to an extension and transfiguration hereafter.

Hence the importance in catechesis of personal, moral commitments in keeping with the Gospel, of

Christian attitudes to the world, be they heroic or very simple; we call them the Christian or evangelical virtues. Hence too, in its efforts to instil the Faith, catechesis will not omit but rather highlight such realities as man's activity for his integral liberation, the search for a society with greater solidarity and fraternity, the fight for justice and the building of peace.[2]

God became incarnate to illuminate as well as to be the meaning of human life. This we need to believe with deep and joyful conviction; this we need to live with constancy and consistency; this we need to proclaim and bear witness to, notwithstanding the tribulations of the times and the hostile ideologies, nearly always so beguiling and unsettling.

And in what way is Jesus the meaning of human existence? He himself explains this with comforting clarity: 'My Father gives you the bread from heaven, the true bread; for the bread of God is the bread which comes down from heaven and gives life to the world … I am the bread of life; no one who comes to me will ever hunger, and no one who believes in me will ever thirst' (John 6:32–35). Jesus is speaking symbolically, referring to the great miracle of the manna, given by God to the Jews when they were going through the desert. Obviously Jesus does not eliminate our ordinary concern about and quest for our daily food and for everything that can make human life more advanced, more up-to-date, more satisfying. But life inevitably passes away. Jesus shows us that the true meaning of our earthly existence is in eternity and that all of human history, with its tragedies and joys, must be seen in the perspective of eternity.

On earth, we too, like the Children of Israel, live out the Exodus experience: our 'promised land' is heaven. God did not forsake his people in the wilderness, nor will he forsake us on our earthly pilgrimage. He has given us a 'bread' which is able to sustain us along our way: the 'bread' is Christ. He above all is food for the soul, both in the Holy Scriptures and in the Sacrament of the Eucharist, in which his very self is present.

We need transcendency! We need God's presence in our daily history! Only thus can we find the meaning of life. Yes, and Jesus keeps saying to us all: 'I am the way, the truth and the life' (John 14:6); 'I am the light of the world; anyone who follows me will not be walking in the dark but will have the light of life' (John 8:12); 'Come to me, all you who labour and are overburdened, and I will give you rest!' (Matthew 11:28).[3]

History today and Christian responsibility

What is the general characteristic of the age in which Providence has called us to live? I think we can answer that it is a great spiritual crisis: of the intellect, of religious faith and, consequently, of ordinary life.

We are called to live in this period of ours and to love it, so that we may save it. What, then, are the demands which this imposes on us?

Many past and recent shipwrecks in the Faith and in the consecrated life, and also many present distressing and perplexing situations, have as their origin a crisis of a philosophical type. We need to pay more serious attention to our own cultural formation. The Second Vatican Council insisted on the need for us always to regard St Thomas Aquinas as our master and teacher, since only by the light and on the basis of the 'perennial philosophy' can the very logical and exacting edifice of Christian doctrine be founded. Leo XIII, of venerable memory, in his famous and ever-contemporary encyclical *Aeterni Patris*, admirably confirmed and illustrated the validity of the rational foundation for the Christian faith.

So, today, our first concern should be for the truth, both for our inner need and for our ministry. We cannot sow error, or leave the Faith in the shadow of doubt. The inherited, sociological type of Christian faith is becoming more and more personal, interior and demanding, which is certainly a good thing; but we must have something that we can give to others! We should remember what St Paul wrote to his disciple Timothy: 'Take great care of all that has been entrusted to you. Turn away from godless philosophical discussions and the contradiction of the "knowledge" which is not knowledge at all; by adopting this, some have missed the goal of faith' (1 Timothy 6:20).

The exhortation is especially apt for our own times, when people so thirst for certainty and clarity and yet are so inwardly trapped and tormented. Ideological confusion gives rise to psychologically immature and defective personalities; the teaching thus emerges as uncertain and sometimes wrong. Precisely because of this, the modern world is in breathless search of models, and most of the time it is left disappointed, defeated and humiliated. So we must be mature personalities, who know how to control our feelings, who assume our role as responsible guides for others, and who seek our self-fulfilment in the place and work where we happen to be.

If we are to love our age and save it, we must have calmness and courage to accept things as they are, without dispirited criticisms and without utopian delusions. So you must all commit yourselves to achieving these ideals of 'maturity', by loving what you have to do, by meditation, spiritual reading, examination of conscience, regular recourse to the Sacrament of Penance, and spiritual direction. The Church and modern society need mature personalities: we must be them, with God's help!⁴

The tragedies of history

You have asked me which of humanity's problems

worries me most. It is this one: the people who do not yet know Christ, who have not yet discovered the great truth of God's love; human beings who are going further and further away from the Lord, wanting to grow yet leaving God on the sidelines or even denying that he exists. They are human beings without a Father, and as a result they are without love: orphans, disorientated, capable of keeping on killing people whom they do not regard as their own brothers, and thus preparing their own self-destruction and annihilation. This is why I want young people to pledge themselves again today to being the apostles of a new evangelization, so as to build a civilization of love.[5]

On the horizon of contemporary civilization – especially in the area of technology and science – the signs and symptoms of death have become particularly obvious and frequent. One has only to think of the arms race and of its inherent danger of nuclear self-destruction. Moreover, everyone has become more and more aware of the grave problems facing vast areas of our planet, which are marked by death-dealing poverty and famine. It is a question of problems that are not only economic but also and above all ethical. But on the horizon of our era there are gathering ever darker 'signs of death': a custom has become widely established – in some places it threatens to become almost an institution – of taking the lives of human beings even before they are born, or before they reach the natural point of death. Furthermore, despite many noble efforts for peace, new wars have broken out and are taking place, wars which destroy the lives or the health of hundreds of thousands of people. And how can one fail to mention the attacks against human life by terrorism, organized even on an international scale?[6]

Why have we come to this? Why is humanity threatened to such a degree on our earthly globe? What are the causes of the injustice we see all about us? Why are so many people dying of hunger? So many millions of refugees at this or that frontier? So many cases where elementary human rights are trampled under foot? So many prisons and concentration camps, so much systematic violence and killing of the innocent, so much ill treatment and torture, so many torments inflicted on the human body and the human conscience? And in the midst of all this, there are also young men with countless innocent victims on their conscience, because they have been brainwashed into thinking that planned terrorism is the only way to make the world a better place.

There has been such great progress by human beings – with which no earlier age in history can compare – in the field of science and technology; but why is it that human progress in the mastering of matter has been turned, in so many aspects, against human beings?

Is this state of affairs perhaps irreversible? Can it be changed? Can we manage to change it? What must we do to prevent life – humanity's life now blossoming – from being turned into a graveyard of nuclear death? What must we do, so that the sin of universal injustice does not gain the mastery over us – the sin of despising human beings, of holding human dignity in contempt, despite all these declarations affirming human rights? *What are we to do?*[7]

Commitment to the 'civilization of love'

We live in times of deep and rapid change. Often, as we apprehensively watch what is happening, we wonder: 'Where should we go?' and 'Whom should we go with?' Fear of the unknown and of the future is rife among your various contemporaries. We are tempted to give up, to retire into our shell and to relax in a state that blocks us off from acquiring our full stature as men and women, as intended in the divine plan. We must resist the temptation to lock ourselves into the logic of personal advantage, for this always leads us further from our true identity, until we become unrecognizable, completely oblivious of the 'name'. What name? The name we all bear, that each one of us bears: *child of God*. This name is deeply engraved in our hearts; it is engraved by Jesus all through his Gospel, his being with us through his works and words, and, above all, through his Cross and Resurrection. That name: child of God, sons and daughters of God.

To *arise* means to set out, to set out on a journey of quest and liberation, of struggle against our own selfishness, of openness to our brothers and sisters. Everyone can complete this itinerary of conversion and renewal. Mainly it takes place in the depths of the individual conscience. As St Luke relates in the wonderful parable of the compassionate Father, the prodigal son 'came to his senses and said: I will arise ...' (Luke 15:17–18). We believers are all called to follow this same path: to arise within, inwardly; to arise from sin; to arise from selfishness; to arise from error and direct our steps to God and to our neighbour without delay ...

He it is who says, 'Arise, you and you and you!' He asks you to give up the idols of this world and to choose him: him, the Love that pours total meaning into our existence and invites us to live our youth as a joyful springtime, like this Sicilian spring today; to live this springtime in the exciting experience of the gift: his gift, Christ's gift, the gift offered to each of us, and then the gift of ourselves to him, the gift of ourselves to others and, through others, to him once more. Lo, the prospect of building another civilization, a new civilization: the civilization of love. We are here to make a start in making this great project come true: the civilization of love. This is Jesus' civilization, this is the Church's civilization, this is true Christian civilization, this is your civilization. You must aspire to this civilization, not to any other: the civilization of love ...

The Lord is straight with you; he tells you right out: 'Anyone who is not with me is against me' (Matthew 12:30); he calls you, in a word, to make a clean, uncompromising choice: either him, or other 'masters', other 'shepherds' who seem at first sight to be convincing but turn out later to be deceptive and false. These are the ones who will entice you into the paths of criminality, of drug abuse, of illicit, degrading activities, of empty, superficial pleasures. Firmly resist every deceitful sower of selfishness and violence. And if any one of you by chance should find yourself ensnared in the paths of evil and feel you are lost, having come to your senses, may you find the courage to turn back to the Father's house, like the prodigal son in the Gospel: 'I will arise, I will arise.'[8]

The meaning of suffering and illness

People who approach suffering with a merely human attitude of mind cannot understand what it means and can easily collapse in defeat; at most they may manage to accept it, being gloomily resigned to the inevitable. We Christians, however, being instructed in the Faith, know that suffering can be transformed – if we offer it to God – into an instrument of salvation, and into a sacred way which helps us get to heaven. For a Christian, pain is no reason for gloominess but for joy: the joy of knowing that on the Cross of Christ all suffering has a redemptive value.

Again today the Lord invites us, saying: 'Come to me, all you who labour and are overburdened, and I will give you rest' (Matthew 11:28). So turn your gaze to him in the sure hope that he will give you relief, that in him you will find solace. Do not be afraid of showing him your sufferings, and at times your loneliness too. Offer him this daily tally of small and often big crosses, and so – even though they often seem unbearable to you – they will not weigh you down, for Christ himself will be carrying them for you: 'For ours were the sufferings he was bearing, ours the sorrows he was carrying' (Isaiah 53:4).

As you follow Christ along this road, you will feel the inner joy of doing God's will. A joy which is compatible with pain, because it is the joy of God's children, who know themselves to be called to follow Jesus more closely on his road to Golgotha.[9]

Whoever follows Christ, whoever accepts St Paul's theology of pain, knows that to suffering there is linked a precious grace, a divine favour, even though this grace remains a mystery for us, since it is hidden under the appearances of a painful fate. In suffering, it is certainly not easy to detect God's authentic love that wills, by suffering which is accepted, to raise human life to the level of Christ's sacrifice. Yet faith makes us cling to this mystery and, despite all, puts peace and joy into the sufferer's soul. Sometimes, with St Paul, we can manage to say: 'In all our

tribulation, I am filled with encouragement and over-
flowing with joy' (1 Corinthians 7:4).[10]

In the perspectives of faith, illness assumes a higher
nobility and has a particular efficacy as an aid to the
apostolic ministry. In this sense, the Church does not
hesitate to declare that she needs the sick and their
oblation to the Lord, so as to obtain more abundant
graces for the whole community. If, in the light of the
Gospel, illness can be a time of grace, a time in which
divine love penetrates more deeply into those who
suffer, there is no doubt that, by their offering, the
sick and inform sanctify themselves and contribute
to the sanctification of others.

This is true particularly for those who devote
themselves to caring for the sick and infirm. This
kind of service is a way of sanctification, like illness
itself. Throughout the centuries, it has been one
manifestation of Christ's charity, he indeed being the
source of all holiness.

It is a service requiring dedication, patience and
tact, combined with a great capacity for compassion
and understanding; all the more so since, besides care
of a strictly medical type, the sick also need to be
given moral support, as Jesus implies: 'I was sick ...
and you visited me' (Matthew 25:36).[11]

Death: its meaning and reality

This life is not a whole, definitively enclosed

between the day we are born and the day we die. It is open to final completion in God. Each of us is painfully aware of life's ending, of the limitations imposed by death. Each of us is in some way conscious of the fact that human beings are not completely contained within these limits and that we cannot die entirely. Too many questions are unasked and too many problems are unsolved – if not in the dimension of personal, individual life, then at least in that of the life of human communities. Families, nations, the human race itself all cease at the moment of the death of Everyman. For none of us lives alone. Through each of us pass various circles.

Christ accepted the full reality of human dying. And this was because he had accomplished a fundamental revolution in the way of understanding what life is. He showed that life is a passing, not only to the bounds of death, but to a new life. For us, as a result, the Cross has become the supreme Chair in Truth about God and human beings. Term in, term out, we all ought to be scholars of this professorship. Then we shall grasp how the Cross is also the cradle of the new human being.

Those who are its scholars look on life like this – they perceive it like this. And this is what they teach others. This meaning of life they stamp on all temporal reality: on morality, creativity, culture, politics, economics.[12]

Judgement after death

The fundamental 'matter' for judgement will be the works of charity which we have done to our neighbour. Christ actually identifies himself with our neighbour. 'In so far as you did this to one of the least of these brothers of mine, you did it to me'; 'In so far as you neglected to do this ... you neglected to do it to me' (Matthew 25:40–45).

According to this text from Matthew, each of us will be judged above all *on love*. But there is no doubt that we shall also be judged *on our faith*: 'If anyone openly declares himself for me in the presence of human beings, the Son of man will declare himself for him in the presence of God's angels.' 'If anyone is ashamed of me and of my words, of him the Son of man will be ashamed when he comes in his own glory and in the glory of the Father' (Luke 12:8; 9:26; Mark 8:38).

From the Gospel, then, we learn one of the basic truths of our religion – that is, that God is the judge of all mankind, finally, universally, and that this power has been handed over by the Father to the Son in close connection with his saving mission. The words said by Jesus during his night-time conversation with Nicodemus attest this with peculiar eloquence: 'God sent his Son into the world not to judge the world, but so that through him the world might be saved' (John 3:17).

Now, of course, Christ is and presents himself

mainly as the *Saviour*. He does not regard it as his mission to judge human beings in accordance with purely human principles. Before all else, he is the One who teaches the way of salvation, and not the accuser of the guilty: 'Do not imagine that I am going to accuse you before the Father; Moses will be the one who accuses you ... since it was about me that he was writing' (John 5:45–46). In what, then, does the judgement consist? Jesus replies: 'The judgement is this: though the light has come into the world, people have preferred darkness to the light, because their deeds were evil' (John 3:19).

Hence it must be said that, in the presence of this Light which is God revealed in Christ, in the presence of this Truth, in a sense our own deeds pass judgement on us. God's will to save human beings has its absolute manifestation in Christ's words and deeds, right through the Gospel to the paschal mystery of the Cross and the Resurrection. And at the same time this becomes the deepest foundation, so to speak, the central criterion of judgement on human deeds and consciences. In this sense above all, 'the Father has entrusted all judgement to the Son' (John 5:22); in him the Father offers everyone the possibility of salvation.

In this same sense, alas! we are already condemned when we reject the opportunity he offers us: 'No one who believes in him will be condemned; but whoever does not believe is condemned already' (John 3:18).

Not believing actually means *rejecting* the salvation which is offered us in Christ ('That person does not believe in the Name of God's only Son'). The same truth is hinted at in ancient Simeon's prophecy recorded in Luke's Gospel, where he proclaimed of Christ: 'He is destined for the fall and for the rise of many in Israel.' The same may be said of the reference to 'the stone which the builders rejected' (Luke 2:34; 20:17–18).[13]

The resurrection and glorification of the body

The glorification of the body, as the eschatological fruit of its divinizing spiritualization, will reveal the ultimate importance of what, from the beginning, was to be a distinguishing sign of the created person in the visible world, and also a means of communicating person-to-person, and an authentic expression of the truth and love through which *communio personarum* is constructed. That permanent significance of the human body, on which the existence of each individual, burdened with an inheritance of concupiscence, has inevitably imposed a series of limitations, struggles and sufferings, is then revealed anew, and is revealed at once in such simplicity and splendour that everyone who shares in 'the other world' will rediscover in his or her glorified body the fountain of the freedom of the gift. With that gift, the perfect 'freedom of the children of God' (cf. Romans 8:14) will also nourish each of those fellowships which will compose the grand community of the communion of saints.[14]

Though before Michelangelo's Last Judgement we stand dazed by splendour and fear, marvelling on the one hand at the glorified bodies, and on the other hand at those sentenced to eternal damnation, we understand too that this entire vision is deeply pervaded by a unique light and a unique artistic logic: the light and logic of the faith proclaimed by the Church when she confesses: 'I believe in one God ... maker of heaven and earth ... of all things visible and invisible.' On the basis of this logic, in the sphere of the light which comes from God, the human body too retains its splendour and its dignity. Once detached from this dimension, to some degree it becomes an object which can very easily get debased, for only before the eyes of God can the human body stay naked and uncovered and yet retain its splendour and beauty intact.[15]

VI

EVIL

Here we find ourselves at the very centre
of what could be called the 'anti-Word',
that is to say 'the anti-Truth'.
For the truth about humanity becomes falsified:
who human beings are and what the impassable
limits of their being and freedom are.

When we are faced with the reality of evil, our questions multiply and we feel anguish. Why does evil exist? Where does it come from? What is the point of it? Why is history full of it?

Sometimes this anguish overtakes a believer, who finds it hard to reconcile so much human suffering on earth with God's absolute and provident goodness. For evil is mysterious in its origin, in its continual and tormenting persistence, and in its terrible consequences in time and, for some people, also in eternity.

For the non-believer, evil is an inexplicable, deplorable, implacable absurdity that cannot be got rid of. For the Christian, evil remains a 'mystery', forming part of the infinite mystery of God himself, Creator and Redeemer. For God permits evil (it is the tares which grow in the field of history and which are not to be uprooted); God is actually subject to physical evil and spiritual suffering; God redeems evil and brings good out of evil, wishing to express his love by means of compassion and forgiveness too.

Original righteousness and original sin

Original righteousness pertains to the mystery of our 'original state', from which, 'historically', we became separated by committing the original sin. Which does not, however, mean that we cannot approach that mystery by means of our theological knowledge. As human beings living in history, we seek to under-stand the mystery of original righteousness, as it were, by its opposite – that is to say, by going back to the experience of our own guilt and our own sinful-ness. We seek to understand original righteousness as an essential characteristic for the theology of the body, starting from the experience of shame, for so the text of the Scriptures itself directs us. Original righteousness, therefore, is that which radically – that is to say, to its very roots – excludes shame of the body in relations between the sexes, eliminating the need for it in human beings, in their hearts, or rather in their consciences.[1]

Human beings, under the influence of the 'father of lies', have become divorced from participation in this. To what degree? Certainly not to the degree of the sin of a pure spirit, to the degree of the sin of Satan. The human spirit is incapable of reaching such a degree. In the very description given in Genesis it is easy to see the difference of degree between the 'breath of evil' on the part of the one who 'has sinned (or remains in sin) from the beginning' and already 'has been judged', and the evil of disobedience on the part of humanity.

Man's disobedience, nevertheless, always means a turning away from God, and in a certain sense the closing up of human freedom in his regard. It also means a certain opening of this freedom – of the human mind and will – to the one who is the 'father of lies'. This act of conscious choice is not only 'disobedience' but also involves a certain consent to the motivation which was contained in the first temptation to sin and which is increasingly renewed during the whole history of humanity on earth: 'For God knows that when you eat of it your eyes will be opened, and you will be like God, knowing good and evil.'

Here we find ourselves at the very centre of what could be called the 'anti-Word', that is to say the 'anti-Truth'. For the truth about humanity becomes falsified – that is, who human beings are and what the impassable limits of their being and freedom are. This 'anti-Truth' is possible because at the same time there is a complete falsification of the truth about who God is. God the Creator is placed in a state of suspicion, indeed of accusation, in the mind of the creature. For the first time in human history there appears the perverse 'genius of suspicion'. He seeks to 'falsify' Good itself, the absolute Good, which precisely in the work of creation has manifested itself as the Good which gives in an inexpressible way: as *bonum diffusivum sui*, as creative love. Who can completely 'convince concerning sin' or concerning this motivation of humanity's original disobedience, except the One who alone is the gift and the source of all giving of gifts – that is, the Spirit, who 'searches the depths of God', and is the love of the Father and the Son?[2]

The sin against the Holy Spirit

Against the background of what has been said so far, certain other words of Jesus, striking and disturbing ones, become easier to understand. We might call them the words of 'unforgiveness'. They are reported for us by the Synoptics in connection with a particular sin which is called 'blasphemy against the Holy Spirit'. This is how they are reported in their three versions:

Matthew: 'Whoever says a word against the Son of man will be forgiven; but whoever speaks against the Holy Spirit will not be forgiven, either in this age or in the age to come' (Matthew 12:13).

Mark: 'All sins will be forgiven the sons of men and whatever blasphemies they utter; but whoever blasphemes against the Holy Spirit never has forgiveness, but is guilty of an eternal sin' (Mark 3:28).

Luke: 'Every man who speaks a word against the Son of man will be forgiven; but he who blasphemes against the Holy Spirit will not be forgiven' (Luke 12:10).

Why is blasphemy against the Holy Spirit unforgivable? How should this be understood? Saint Thomas Aquinas replies that it is a question of a sin that is 'unforgivable by its very nature, in so far as it excludes the elements through which the forgiveness of sin takes place.'

According to such an exegesis, 'blasphemy' does not properly consist in offending against the Holy Spirit in words; it consists rather in the refusal to accept the salvation which God offers to us through the Holy Spirit, working through the power of the Cross. If we reject the 'convincing concerning sin' which comes from the Holy Spirit and which has the power to save, we also reject the 'coming' of the Counsellor – that 'coming' which was accomplished in the Paschal Mystery, in union with the redemptive power of Christ's blood: the blood that 'purifies the conscience from dead works'.

We know that the result of such a purification is the forgiveness of sins. Therefore, whoever rejects the Spirit and the Blood remains in 'dead works', in sin.

And the blasphemy against the Holy Spirit consists precisely in the radical refusal to accept this forgiveness, of which he is the intimate giver and which presupposes the genuine conversion which he brings about in the conscience.[3]

The threefold concupiscence and passion

The lust of the flesh and with it the lust of the eyes and the pride of life are 'in the world' and at the same time 'come from the world', not as fruit of the mystery of creation, but as fruit of the tree of the knowledge of good and evil (cf. Genesis 2:17). That which comes to fruit in the threefold lust is not the 'world' created by God for mankind; the fundamental 'goodness' of this world we have often read about in Genesis 1: 'God saw that it was good ... It was very good.' What instead comes to fruit in the threefold lust is the breach of the first covenant with the Creator, with God Elohim, with God Yahweh. This covenant was broken in the human heart. Here we should really make an accurate analysis of the events described in Genesis 3:1–6. We will, however, only refer in general terms to the mystery of sin at the outset of human history. For only as the result of sin, as fruit of the breach of the covenant with God in the human heart – in the depths of the human soul – did the 'world' of the Book of Genesis become the 'world' of the Johannine words (1 John 2:15–16): the place and source of concupiscence.[4]

By stifling the voice of conscience, passion brings with it a restlessness of the body and the senses: this is the restlessness of the 'outer person'. When the 'inner person' has been reduced to silence, passion – having, so to speak, obtained freedom of action – manifests itself as an insistent inclination to satisfy the senses and the body.

According to the criterion of the individual whom passion sways, this gratification ought to put out the fire. On the contrary, however, it does not reach the sources of inner peace; it only affects the outer level of the human personality.

Passion aims at gratification; so it blunts thoughtful activity and disregards the voice of conscience; thus, having no principle of 'indestructibility' within itself, it 'wears itself out'. The dynamism of use is inherent in it and this tends to get exhausted. True, where passion finds a place in the ensemble of the profoundest energies of the spirit, it can also become a creative force; but for this to happen, it has to undergo a radical transformation. If instead it stifles the deepest energies of heart and conscience (as we read in the description in Ecclesiasticus 23:17–22), 'it is consumed' and in it, at first remove, the person who falls prey to it is consumed too.[5]

The strife between flesh and Spirit

The 'flesh' in the language of St Paul's letters means not only the 'outer' person but also the person who is 'inwardly' subject to the 'world' – that is to say, confined within the limits of those values belonging only to the world and of those aims which the world is able to impose on us: values to which we are, in so far as we are 'flesh', precisely susceptible. Thus Paul's language seems connected to the essential content of John, and the language of both denotes that which is defined by various terms in modern ethics and anthropology – for instance, 'humanistic autarchy', 'secularism', or even, in a general sense, 'sensualism'. People who live 'according to the flesh' are disposed only to that which comes 'from the world'; they are people of the 'senses', people of the threefold concupiscence. Their deeds confirm this.

This type of person lives, as it were, at the opposite pole from what 'the Spirit wills'. The Spirit of God wills something different from what the flesh wills, yearns for something different from what the flesh yearns for: something already deep in the human heart, at the inner source of human acts and aspirations – 'so that you cannot do the things that you would' (Galatians 5:17).

The tension between the 'flesh' and the 'Spirit' is basically immanent, even if not confined to this level. It takes form in the human heart as a 'battle' between good and evil. The desire of which Christ speaks in the Sermon on the Mount (cf. Matthew 5:27–28), for all that it is an 'interior' act, is nonetheless – in Pauline language – a manifestation of life 'according to the flesh'. At the same time, this desire allows us to see how, within us, life 'according to the flesh' conflicts with life 'according to the Spirit', and how the latter, in our present state, given our hereditary sinfulness, is constantly exposed to the weakness and inadequacy of the former, to which we must often give way if not inwardly strengthened to do exactly that 'which the Spirit wills'. From this we can deduce that Paul's words dealing with life 'according to the flesh' and 'according to the Spirit' are at once a synthesis and a programme; and this is how we need to understand them.[6]

It is significant that Paul, speaking of the 'works of the flesh' (cf. Galatians 5:11-21), mentions not only 'sexual vice, impurity, sensuality … drunkenness, orgies' – hence everything that, according to an objective way of thinking, has the character of 'carnal sins' and of sensual pleasure connected with the flesh – but he names other sins too, to which we should not otherwise be inclined to attribute a 'carnal' and 'sensual' character: 'worship of false gods, sorcery, antagonisms, rivalry, jealousy, bad temper, quarrels, disagreements, factions, malice …' (Galatians 5:20-21). In accordance with our own anthropological (and ethical) categories, we should be more inclined to call all the 'works' listed here 'sins of the human spirit', even though they are sins of the 'flesh'. Not without reason would we have been able to detect in them the effects of 'lust of the eyes' or of 'the

pride of life', rather than those of the 'lust of the flesh'.
Paul, however, qualifies them all as 'works of the flesh'.
This is to be understood exclusively against the background of that ampler, in a sense metonymical, meaning which the term 'flesh' takes on in St Paul's letters,
being contrasted not only and not so much with the
human 'spirit' as with the 'Holy Spirit' who works in
the human soul (the human spirit).'

Victory over evil

In Christ, evil is already conquered, death has been
defeated in its very root, which is sin. Christ has
descended into the depths of the human heart with
that most potent of weapons: love, which is stronger
than death (cf. Song of Songs 8:6). And so, we Christians – and even more so, we, God's ministers – do
not advance into history with uncertain stride. We
cannot do so, for we have been ransomed from 'the
power of darkness' (Colossians 1:13); we advance
along the right road 'in the inheritance of the saints
in light' (Colossians 1:12). And so, whatever uncertainty may lie in wait for us, whatever temptations
affecting ourselves or our mission and ministry, these
can be overcome in this wonderful perspective of
union with Christ, in whom everything is possible
for us, since he is our final victory. In him are the
beginning and root of our personal victory, in him
we find the strength we need for overcoming any
difficulty that may arise, since for us the Lord is

'wisdom, righteousness, holiness and redemption'
(1 Corinthians 1:30).[8]

The right use of freedom

Paul puts us on guard against the possibility of making a wrong use of freedom, a use conflicting with the liberation of the human spirit achieved by Christ and countermanding that freedom wherewith 'Christ has made us free'. For Christ realized and displayed the freedom that finds its fulfilment in charity, the freedom owing to which we are 'at the service of one another'; in other words, the freedom that becomes the source of new 'works' and of 'life' according to the Spirit. The antithesis and, in a sense, the denial of this use of freedom takes place when it becomes 'an excuse for living according to the flesh' for us. For then freedom becomes a source of 'works' and 'life' according to the flesh. It ceases to be that genuine freedom wherewith 'Christ has made us free' and becomes 'an excuse for living according to the flesh', the source (or rather the instrument) of a specific 'yoke' from the pride of life, the lust of the eyes and the lust of the flesh. So people who live 'according to the flesh', that is to say, who subject themselves – even if not entirely consciously but nonetheless effectively – to the threefold concupiscence and particularly to the lust of the flesh, cease to be capable of that freedom wherewith 'Christ has made us free', cease also to be fit for the true self-giving which is the fruit and expression of this freedom. They also cease to be capable of that gift which is connected with the spousal significance of the human body, with which we dealt in our earlier analyses of the Book of Genesis (cf. Genesis 2:23–25).[9]

The Sacrament of Penance

Forgiveness of sins, experienced for the first time in Baptism, is a constant necessity in every Christian's life. Re-establishing an adequate sense of sin is the first step to be achieved, if we are objectively to confront the grave spiritual crisis today looming over men and women: a crisis that we may describe as 'an eclipse of conscience' (Reconciliatio et paenitentia 18). Without a healthy awareness of their own sins, people never experience the depth of God's redeeming love for them while they are still sinners (cf. Romans 5:8). Since the idea is widespread that happiness consists in satisfying ourselves and in being satisfied with ourselves, the Church must even more energetically proclaim that only God's grace, and not therapeutic or self-justificatory models, can heal the conflicts which sin causes in the human heart (cf. Romans 3:24; Ephesians 2:5).

For Catholics in a state of mortal sin, individual, integral confession, with respective absolution, is still the only ordinary way for the faithful to be reconciled with God and with the Church (cf. Catechism of the Catholic Church 1484; Codex of Canon

Law, can. 960; *Reconciliatio et paenitentia* 17). The Divine Physician's words of absolution – 'your sins are forgiven' (Mark 2:5) – said by the priest acting *in persona Christi Capitis* are addressed personally to the individual penitent. Any exceptions to this practice are governed by conditions of *gravis necessitas,* which are required for the granting of general absolution (*Codex of Canon Law,* can. 961; cf. *Catechism of the Catholic Church* 1483), understood in accordance with the Church's clearly expressed view in this respect.[10]

Purify your hearts in the Sacrament of Reconciliation. They lie who say that the Church's invitation to repent comes from a 'repressive' mentality. Sacramental Confession is not repression but liberation; it does not revive feelings of guilt, but wipes guilt out; it cancels the evil committed and bestows the grace of forgiveness. The causes of evil are not to be sought outside us but above all within our hearts; and the remedy too begins from the heart. So Christians, being sincere in their pledge of conversion, ought to revolt against human standardization, and by the lives they lead should proclaim the joy of true liberation from sin through Christ's forgiveness.

To those who have given up going to the Sacrament of Reconciliation and compassionate love, I make this appeal: *Come back to this source of grace; don't be afraid!* Christ himself is waiting for you. He will heal you, and you will be at peace with God!

To all young people in the Church I address a special invitation to receive Christ's forgiveness and strength in the Sacrament of Penance. It is a sign of strength to be able to say: 'I have made a mistake; I have sinned, Father; I have offended you, my God; I'm sorry; I ask your forgiveness; I will try again, since I trust in your strength and believe in your forgiveness. And I know that the power of your Son's Paschal Mystery – the Death and Resurrection of our Lord Jesus Christ – is greater than my weaknesses and all the sins in the world. I will come and confess my sins, and I shall be healed and shall live in your love!'[11]

VII

WORK

Work should help human beings
to become better,
more mature spiritually, more responsible,
so that they can fulfil their vocation
on earth both as unique individuals
and in the community with others,
but above all in that fundamental
human community:
the family

By meditating on the Omnipotence and Omniscience of God the Creator and Lord of humanity and the cosmos, we may deduce that God in fact wished to create human beings endowed with intelligence and will-power, so that they could collaborate with him in giving and improving life by work, study, science and art.

God could have created everything directly; yet instead he created, on the one hand, human intelligence and, on the other, the cosmos to be studied, discovered, used and improved. Seen thus, all work, however humble, however hidden, is collaboration with God, and hence it is a cause of great dignity and a source of supreme inner satisfaction.

Daily physical reality, however, teaches that sometimes work is enjoyable and congenial, hence rewarding and satisfying, but at other times wearisome, frustrating and unpleasant. Work often involves danger to life; at other times it is done out of pure necessity to survive, or in conditions which are unjust, humiliating and exploitative.

Sometimes work is replaced by the terrible phenomenon of unemployment, and then what should, metaphysically speaking, be a great dignity and a supreme ideal becomes instead a torment, a nightmare and desolation.

The value and dignity of labour

Faithful to her Divine Founder, the Church has always respected and promoted the dignity of labour. And she has done this by insisting on the fundamental role played by human work in God's designs; she has done this by applauding the goals which human intelligence has managed to reach, especially in the field of science and technology; she has done this by showing her preference for all workers and particularly for those whose work is especially tiring, such as those who work in factories or on farms; she has done this by granting and protecting their petitions, their interests and their legitimate aspirations; she has done this by drawing near to the world of labour, in their 'shanty towns', in their humble hovels, or in their comfortable housing, to help them materially and spiritually, to save them from all kinds of danger, to protect their moral and social sense, and to improve their living conditions.[1]

Work is the fundamental dimension of human life on earth. For human beings, work has not only a technical but also an ethical significance. We may say we 'subject' the earth to ourselves when we, by the way we behave, become its lord rather than its slave, and when we also become the lord and not the slave of work.

Work should help human beings to become better, more mature spiritually, more responsible, so that they can fulfil their vocation on earth as unique individuals and in the community with others, but above all in that fundamental human community: the family. Men and women, uniting together in this very community, whose character the Creator himself established at the beginning of the world, give life to new human beings. Work should enable this human community to find the means necessary for developing properly and earning a living.[2]

Let work never be to the detriment of human beings! By now it is recognized on all sides that technical progress is not accompanied by adequate respect for humanity. While wonderful in its continuous conquests, technology has often had the effect of impoverishing people in their essential humanity, by depriving them of their inner, spiritual dimension and stifling their sense of true and higher values. We need to restore the primacy of the spiritual! The Church invites you to preserve a proper scale of values. Let the famous Benedictine dual concept, *Ora et labora*, be for you, my brothers and sisters, an inexhaustible source of true wisdom, of sure equilibrium, of human perfection. May prayer give wings to your work, purify your intentions, and defend you from the perils of boredom and carelessness; and may your work, after your exertions, allow you to rediscover the invigorating force of the encounter with God, in whom we once more recover our true, great stature. *Ora et labora!*[3]

According to the Council (*Lumen gentium* 41), work constitutes a road to holiness, because it offers an opportunity for:

(a) *Self-improvement*. Work develops the human personality by exercising its qualities and potentialities. We understand this better today, with the tragedy of the many unemployed who feel themselves diminished in their dignity as human beings. The greatest emphasis must be laid on this personal dimension for all workers, in an effort to ensure at all costs worthy working conditions for human beings.

(b) *Helping our fellow-citizens*. This is the social dimension of labour, which is a service for the good of all. This orientation should always be emphasized: labour is not a self-centred activity but an altruistic one; we do not work exclusively for ourselves, but for others too.

(c) *Improving society at large and the creation*. Work then gains a historical-eschatological, we might say cosmic, dimension, in that its purpose is to contribute towards improving material conditions of life and the world, by helping mankind, by these means, to reach the higher goals to which God is calling us. Labour's orientation towards the goal of improvement on a universal scale is made more obvious by our progress today. But much still remains to be done if we are to adjust labour to those ends which are willed by the Creator.

(d) *Imitating Christ* in active charity.[4]

The Church and the social question

Evangelization, the Church's task in every age and clime, inevitably affects the life of human society. The Church cannot be restricted to her temples, any more than God can be confined to human awareness. Faithful to her redemptive mission, the Church seeks to draw all human beings nearer to God, and in so doing she increases the dignity of human beings, since she seeks to make them like Jesus Christ. For this reason, she calls on all Christians, by virtue of their sharing in Christ's mission and as members of the Church, to do everything in their power to affirm and defend the dignity of their fellow human beings, with all the spiritual and material consequences of that dignity in the lives of each individual and of society as a whole. She calls for this, since it is the Lord's will that 'You must love one another just as I have loved you' (John 13:34). This love for others is what distinguishes Christ's disciples (cf. John 13:35) and will make them deserving of eternal reward or punishment (cf. Matthew 25:31–46).[5]

Not only does the Church exhort us to be good but, with her social teaching, she is anxious to enlighten people and show them the direction they should follow in their lawful quest for happiness, and guide them to discover the truth amid the non-stop offerings of today's dominant ideologies. The Christian postulate is characterized by optimism and hope, since it is based on the human being and, from a sound humanism, seeks to make itself heard in social, political and economic institutions. It is inspired by the human being and regards the human being as the protagonist in building society. But we are talking – and this should always be borne in mind – about human beings who have been created in the image and likeness of their Creator and called to mould this image into their individual and community lives. We

are talking, in effect, about an optimism which is realistic and non-utopian, since it is aware of the ever-per-
nicious existence of sin, manifesting itself too in the
structures which, instead of serving humanity, turn
against it. And for this very reason, an ambivalence
comes to light which makes of all reality a possible
instrument for the bringing about of God's plan or,
contrariwise, an obstacle to the same, caused by
human selfishness and the presence of evil.[6]

The Church's social doctrine is not a 'third way'
between liberal capitalism and Marxist collectivism,
nor even a possible alternative to other solutions less
radically opposed to one another: rather, it constitutes a category of its own. Nor is it an ideology, but
rather the accurate formulation of the results of a
careful reflection on the complex realities of human
existence, in society and in the international order, in
the light of faith and of the Church's tradition. Its
main aim is to interpret these realities, determining
their conformity with or divergence from the lines of
the Gospel teaching on man and his vocation, a vocation which is at once earthly and transcendent; its
aim is thus to guide Christian behaviour. It therefore
belongs to the field, not of ideology, but of theology
and particularly of moral theology.

The teaching and spreading of her social doctrine
are part of the Church's evangelizing mission. And
since it is a doctrine aimed at guiding people's

behaviour, it consequently gives rise to a commitment to justice, in accordance with each individual's role, vocation and circumstances.[7]

Solidarity

Solidarity helps us to see the 'other' – whether a person, people or nation – not just as some kind of instrument, with a work capacity and physical strength to be exploited at low cost and then discarded when no longer useful, but as our 'neighbour', a 'helper' (cf. Genesis 2:18–20), to be made a sharer, on a par with ourselves, in the banquet of life to which all are equally invited by God. Hence the importance of reawakening the religious awareness of individuals and peoples.

The solidarity which we propose is the path to peace and at the same time to development. For world peace is inconceivable unless the world's leaders come to recognize that interdependence in itself demands the abandonment of the politics of blocs, the sacrifice of all forms of economic, military or political imperialism, and the transformation of mutual distrust into collaboration. This is precisely the act proper to solidarity among individuals and nations.

Solidarity is undoubtedly a Christian virtue. In what has been said so far it has been possible to identify many points of contact between solidarity and charity, which is the distinguishing mark of Christ's disciples (cf. John 13:35).

In the light of faith, solidarity seeks to go beyond itself, to take on the specifically Christian dimensions of total gratuity, forgiveness and reconciliation. One's neighbour is then not only a human being with his or her own rights and a fundamental equality with everyone else, but becomes the living image of God the Father, redeemed by the blood of Jesus Christ and placed under the permanent action of the Holy Spirit. One's neighbour must therefore be loved, even if an enemy, with the same love with which the Lord loves him or her; and for that person's sake one must be ready for sacrifice, even the ultimate one: to lay down one's life for the brethren (cf. 1 John 3:16).

At that point, awareness of the common fatherhood of God, of the brotherhood of all in Christ – 'children in the Son' – and of the presence and life-giving action of the Holy Spirit will bring to our vision of the world a new criterion for interpreting it. Beyond human and natural bonds, already so close and strong, there is discerned in the light of faith a new model of the unity of the human race, which must ultimately inspire our solidarity.[8]

Economic development

No genuine development can be based on economic profit alone, for this, if it becomes absolute, leads to corruption. It is essential that the entire civil community grow and be based on strong moral values, and the source of such values, as you well know, is spiritual! Only the light of conscience and of the moral law allows solutions to be found which are equal to the grave questions to be met in everyday life and in the way society is organized.[9]

All too often, an exclusivist economic logic, further perverted by a crass materialism, has invaded every field of existence, jeopardizing the environment, threatening the family and destroying any respect for the human person. Factories spew out their rubbish, disfiguring and contaminating the environment and making the air unbreathable. Waves of immigrants are crowded together in unworthy hovels, where many lose hope and end their days in misery. Children, youngsters, adolescents, find no living space in which to develop their physical and spiritual energies to the full, all too often cooped up in unhealthy surroundings or forced on to the street amid surging traffic, concrete buildings and the anonymity of the heedless crowd. Next to parts of the city where people live with all modern conveniences, are other areas where the most elementary things are lacking; and settlements on the outskirts proliferate beyond control. All too often development turns into a gigantic version of the parable of Dives and Lazarus. The close proximity of luxury and extreme poverty accentuates the sense of frustration in the disinherited. Here a fundamental question has to be asked: how can the city be transformed into a truly human place, as to its natural environment, its buildings and institutions?

An essential condition for this is to give the economy a human direction and logic. And what has been said about work applies here too. We have to set the various fields of existence free from being dominated by an overpowering economism. We must put the demands of the economy in their right place and create a multiform social fabric to prevent standardization. No one is excused from working at this task. We can all do something, in ourselves and around us. Is it not possibly true that the most deprived areas are often the places where solidarity evokes gestures of outstanding selflessness and generosity? Christians, wherever you are, assume your responsibilities in this immense effort to restructure the city in human terms. Your religion makes this a duty. Faith and experience together will give you the light and energy for setting to work.[10]

The significance and interpretation of capitalism

If the term 'capitalism' means an economic system which recognizes the fundamental and positive role of business, the market, private property and the resulting responsibility for the means of production, as well as free human creativity in the economic sector, then the answer is certainly in the affirmative ... But if 'capitalism' means a system in which freedom in the economic sector is not circumscribed with a strong juridical framework which places it at the service of human freedom in its totality, and which sees it as a particular aspect of that freedom, the core of which is ethical and religious, then the reply is certainly negative.[11]

For the sole criterion to be profit is not good enough, especially if this criterion were to be erected into an absolute: 'making more' to 'own more', and not only tangible objects but financial partnerships, allowing ever more extensive and ever more commanding forms of ownership.

Not that the profit motive is in itself unjust. A business could not succeed without it. A reasonable search for profit is, anyhow, consistent with the right to 'economic initiative'. What I mean to say is only that, to be 'just', the profit must be subject to moral criteria, particularly to those consistent with the principle of solidarity.

The law of profit and the demands of an ever more exhausting business commitment can never replace the duty which every man and every woman has to be open to their family, neighbour, culture, society and, above all else, to their God. This many-sided availability to higher values on the part of the individual will certainly help to confer true meaning and just measure on that same commercial activity.

An important task for the Christian businessman,

but also for all who have people's real good at heart today, would be to establish a scale of priorities, as it were, of the goods to be produced. For not all goods are equally useful and necessary. Here the criterion of solidarity and the common good can be brought into sharper focus, making it easier for us to grasp that certain products have a closer relation to the '*being*' of the human person, while others only serve its '*having*', and hence as such are worth less from the human point of view, whatever their market value may be. Multiplying these latter products, with an excessive and artificial substitution of newer and newer but instantly obsolete models, is what we call 'consumerism' (cf. *Sollicitudo rei socialis* 28). No business should aim to create superfluous needs, so as then to try to satisfy them with more and more sophisticated products, which in turn cause new needs.[12]

More and more countries are victims of exploitation in the context of current and international economic systems. Less and less is paid for the products of hard work on the land, while more and more is demanded for what is produced by industrial activity. In this way, instead of development, to which they have a right, many nations are, as it were, condemned to stagnation, unemployment and emigration. We are talking of an unjust system which today is becoming a world problem: it is an injustice to be laid at the door of the so-called First World, *vis–à–vis* the deteriorating conditions of peoples in the Third World. Isn't the fundamental order guaranteeing the priority of labour over capital being disturbed on a grand scale? Won't capital perhaps become more and more powerful and inhuman? And the victims of conditions of this sort are increasingly the individual and the family.[13]

The tragedy of unemployment

Thus, your first and fundamental aspiration is to work. What suffering, what hardship and misery unemployment causes! So the first and fundamental concern of all and each – government officials, politicians, trade union leaders and owners of businesses – should be this: to give work to all. To expect the problem to be solved as the more or less automatic result of an economic order and development, be these what they may, in which employment materializes as a secondary consequence, is unrealistic and hence inadmissable. Economic theory and practice should have the guts to consider employment and its modern possibilities as a central element among their objectives.[14]

Central to all thinking about the world of labour and the economy must always be the human being. To fulfil all the objective requirements of justice, respect for the intangible dignity of the human person must always be the decisive factor – and not only that of the individual worker, but of his family too; not only of the people of today, but also of the generations to come.

Also, from this principle – which today, even more than in the past, demands a change of thought – comes light for understanding the problems of your countries, which I can mention only briefly here but which concern me very much.

I think, for instance, of those whose jobs are at risk or even have already been lost. After very accurate investigation, a restructuring of groups may show itself to be needed; and the more calmly this can be envisaged, the better things will be. However, the workers who have given of their best over many years must on no account be the only people to suffer the disadvantages of this![15]

VIII

THE WORLD

It isn't difficult to see how the world today,
its beauty and grandeur notwithstanding,
the conquests of science and technology
notwithstanding,
the sought-after and abounding material goods it
has to offer notwithstanding,
is thirsty for more truth, more love, more joy.

*Humanity has been willed and created by God, and
hence God wills our history: our first duty is to acknowledge the world in its various forms of expression.*

*Substantially, there are three 'fronts' of knowl-
edge: the cultural front, with its manifold manifestations; the political front, with its continuous,
oscillating happenings; and the religious front.*

*The second fundamental duty is to love the
world – that is, humanity. Certainly, evil must be
condemned and error must be corrected, but our
basic attitude must be one of love, understanding,
pity, kindness and forgiveness.*

The world in the light of God's word

Christ says the Kingdom of Heaven is 'like a dragnet that is cast into the sea and brings in a haul of all kinds of fish' (Matthew 13:47). These simple words completely alter the physiognomy of the world: the physiognomy of our human world as we ourselves make it by experience and science. Experience and science cannot cross the confines of the 'world' and of human existence within it, for these are necessarily linked to the 'sea of time' – the confines of a world in which we live and die in accordance with the words in Genesis: 'Dust you are and to dust you shall return' (Genesis 3:19). Christ's parable, in contrast, speaks of our being transposed into another 'world', into another dimension of our existence. In a word, the Kingdom of Heaven is this new dimension, opening up above the 'sea of time'; at the same time it is the 'dragnet', labouring in this sea for the destiny of the individual and the whole human race in God.[1]

We cannot regard the technological world, our work, as a kingdom completely estranged from the truth. Hence even this world is far from deprived of direction; quite the reverse, it has very definitely improved people's living conditions, and the difficulties caused by the harmful effects of developing a technological civilization do not justify our forgetting the benefits that this same progress has conferred. There are no grounds for conceiving technological, scientific culture as being in opposition to the world of God's creation.

It is perfectly obvious that technological knowledge can be put to good as well as to evil use. People investigating the effects of poison can use their knowledge to cure as well as to kill. But there can be no doubts as to the direction in which we should look, so as to tell what is good from what is evil.

Technological science, directed towards transforming the world, is justified in proportion to the service it performs for the individual and the human race at large.[2]

The Church and the world:
the dangers of the post-Conciliar period

There are two groups I particularly want to recommend to your care as pastors. The first consists of those who, from the impulses of the Second Vatican Council, have drawn the false conclusion that the dialogue with the world, into which the Church has entered, is incompatible with the clear duty of the Magisterium and the norms of the said Church – in a word, with the mandate of the official hierarchy, unequivocally founded on Christ's mission to the Church. Show that both go together: faithfulness to a mission that cannot be set aside, and nearness to humanity, with all its experiences and problems.

The other groups are those who, partly because of inconsistent or too hasty results produced by the

Second Vatican Council, no longer feel at home in the Church of today or who actually intend to leave it. It is important to convey to these people, as firmly as you can but nonetheless with all prudence, that the Church of Vatican II and that of Vatican I and that of Trent and the early Councils is one and the same Church.

Commit yourselves with all your strength to seeing that the indestructible criteria and norms of Christian behaviour are upheld both evidently and attractively in the lives of believers.

A deep breach is opening up between the life-style of a secularized society and the demands of the Gospel. Many people would like to take part in Church life but no longer find any relationship between the world in which they live and Christian principles. It is believed that the Church sticks firmly to her norms only out of rigidity, and that this conflicts with the mercy of which Jesus sets the example in the Gospel. Jesus' hard requests, such as 'Go away, and from this moment sin no more' (John 8:11), get ignored. Often these people fall back on their personal conscience but forget that this conscience is the eye that does not of itself possess light, but only when it looks to the authentic source of light.

Another thing: faced with mechanization, functionalization and organization, the rising generation evinces a deep mistrust of institutions, norms and regulations. The young contrast the Church – her hierarchical constitution, ordered liturgy, dogmas and norms – with the spirit of Jesus. But the spirit needs bases to preserve it and hand it on. Christ himself is the origin of the Church's every mission and every mandate, in which his promise is fulfilled: 'Look, I am with you always; yes, to the end of time' (Matthew 28:20).[3]

The spiritual needs of the world

In knowledge of Christ, you have the Gospel key. In knowledge of Christ, you have a grasp of the world's needs. Inasmuch as he became one of us in all things except sin, your union with Jesus of Nazareth never can and never will be an obstacle to understanding and responding to the needs of the world. And lastly, in knowledge of Christ not only will you discover and understand the limitations of human wisdom and of human solutions to human needs, but you will also experience Jesus' power and the importance of human reason and human strength when these are imbued with Jesus' strength, when these are redeemed in Christ.[4]

Human beings cannot be reduced to the sphere of their material needs. Progress cannot be measured by economic values alone. The human being's spiritual dimension must have its rightful place. Human beings are truly themselves by means of the maturity of their spirit, of their conscience, of their relationship with God and with their neighbour. There will be no better world nor a better ordering of social life, than one giving precedence to these values of the human spirit. Remember this carefully, all those of you who rightly desire changes for a better and more just society; you young people who rightly protest against all the harm, discrimination, violence and agony inflicted on human beings. Remember: the order you desire is a moral order, and you will not achieve it any other way if you do not assure precedence to everything constituting the strength of the human spirit: justice, love, friendship.[5]

Today an invasive materialism is imposing its dominion on us in many different forms and with an aggressiveness sparing no one. The most sacred principles, once a secure guide for the behaviour of the individual and of society, have been completely eliminated by false claims concerning freedom, the sacred character of life, the indissolubility of marriage, the true significance of human sexuality and the right attitude to adopt towards the material benefits offered us by progress.

Today many people are tempted by self-indulgence and consumerism, and people's identity is often defined in terms of what they've got. Prosperity and abundance, the moment they start becoming accessible to wider strata of society, tend to give people the idea that they have a right to everything which prosperity can offer, and to make them more and more self-centred in their demands. Everyone claims complete freedom in all sectors of human behaviour, and new models of morality get put forward in the name of an alleged liberty. When a nation's moral fibre is weakened, when the sense of personal responsibility fades away, then people are willing to justify injustices, and the door is open to violence in all its forms and to the manipulation of the majority by the few. The challenge which is already with us consists in being tempted to accept as true freedom that which in actual fact is only a new form of slavery.

It thus becomes ever more urgent for us to be rooted in the truth that comes from Christ, who is 'the way, the truth and the life' (John 14:6), and in the strength that he himself offers us through his Spirit. Especially in the Eucharist shall we be given the Lord's strength and love.[6]

The moral message of the Church and pluralism

Today's alleged progress is only true progress when it serves the total human being. Besides the material values, this human wholeness of necessity includes spiritual and moral values too.

So it is a very deplorable error – and one that is grave in its consequences – when, as often happens in modern society, a justified pluralism turns into neutrality as to values, and when, in the name of ill-

understood democracy, it comes to be believed that
ethical norms and the use of the moral categories of
right and wrong can be dispensed with more and
more in public life.

In virtue of the prophetic duty handed down to her,
the Church, in the name of truth, cannot fail to stig-
matize as moral guilt or sin everything that obviously
infringes human dignity or God's commandment.
In particular, she cannot be silent when legitimate
human rights as lofty as the right to life, in whatever
form and at whatever stage, are in danger of becoming objects of arbitrary action.

The Church is sent to bear witness to the truth,
and by so doing she makes a valuable contribution to
establishing a social and public life worthy of human
beings. In season, out of season, she reminds the
world of the human being's high dignity and vocation
as God's creature. Recognizable to all, this dignity
shines forth in all its brilliance and grandeur in Jesus
Christ, in his life's message and in his teaching. In
him alone – such is the conviction of our Christian
faith – do we human beings experience the complete
truth about ourselves.[7]

The new evangelization

The new evangelization does not consist in a 'new
gospel', for this would always be derived from ourselves, from our culture, from our own analysis of
human needs. So it would not be a 'gospel' but mere

human invention, and there would be no salvation in it. Nor is it a question of excising everything from the Gospel that might seem hard for today's mentality to accept. Culture is not the measure of the Gospel, but Jesus Christ is the measure of every culture and every human action. No, the new evangelization is not born of a desire 'to please human beings' or to 'win their favour' (cf. Galatians 1:10), but of responsibility for the gift which God has given us in Christ, in whom we have access to the truth about God and human beings and the possibility of authentic life.

The new evangelization has, as its starting point, the certainty that in Christ there are 'unsearchable riches' (cf. Ephesians 3:8) that no culture nor any age can exhaust and to which we human beings can ever have recourse to enrich ourselves (cf. Special Assembly for Europe, Synod of Bishops, *Concluding Declaration* 3). These riches are, first and foremost, Christ himself, his person, because he is our salvation. We human beings of whatever age and culture can, by approaching him through faith and through incorporation into his Body – which is the Church – find answers to these questions, ever old and ever new, with which we face the mystery of our existence and which we bear indelibly printed in our hearts, since the Creation, by the wound of sin.

An evangelization, new in its ardour, postulates a solid faith, an intense pastoral charity and a great faithfulness which, under the action of the Spirit, may generate a mystique, an unrestrainable enthusiasm for the task of preaching the Gospel. In the language of the New Testament, this is the *parrhesia* which inflames the heart of the apostle (cf. Acts 5:28–29; cf. *Redemptoris missio* 45).[8]

The rights of peoples and minorities

Underpinning the universal obligation to understand and respect the diversity and richness of other peoples, other societies, cultures and religions, there are two fundamental principles. First, the inalienable dignity of every human person, regardless of racial, ethnic, cultural or national origins or of religious creed, means that when people unite into groups they have the right to enjoy a collective identity. Hence minorities within a country have the right to exist with their own language, culture and traditions, and the State is morally bound to allow room for their identity and self-expression. Second, the fundamental unity of the human race, drawing its origins from God, the Creator of all things, demands that no group be considered superior to another. Similarly it demands that integration be built on a real solidarity and on freedom from discrimination. Consequently the State has a duty to respect and defend the differences existing between its citizens, and to allow their diversity to serve the common good. Experience shows that peace and internal security can only be guaranteed by respect for the rights of all those who are entrusted to the responsibility of the State.

Seen like this, the freedom of individuals and communities to profess and practise their religion is an essential element for peaceful human coexistence. Freedom of conscience, freedom to seek the truth and to act in accordance with one's own religious faith are so fundamentally human that any attempt to curtail them leads almost inevitably to relentless conflict.

Since nation-states first came into being, the presence of minorities on the same soil has always represented a positive challenge and an opportunity for developing a richer society. In a period of growing awareness about the importance of respect for human rights as the basis for a just and peaceful world, the question of the respect due to minorities ought to be tackled seriously, especially by the political and religious authorities.

In the course of this century, extremely negative experiences regarding the treatment of minorities, especially in Europe, but in other places too, have led the international community to react strongly and to secure the rights of such groups in international agreements. The way in which this intention is translated into the laws and behaviour of each country is a measure of the maturity of that country and a guarantee of its ability to promote peaceful coexistence within its borders and to contribute to the peace of the world.

To guarantee the participation of minorities in

political life is the sign of a morally mature society and does honour to all those nations in which all citizens are free to take part in national life in a climate of justice and peace.[9]

Religious freedom is a right possessed by all, since it is derived from the inalienable dignity of every human being. It exists independently of political and social structures and, as has been affirmed in numerous international documents, the State is duty bound to defend this freedom from attack or interference. Where there is discrimination against citizens on the grounds of their religious convictions, there a fundamental injustice is committed against the human being and against God; and the road that leads to peace is blocked.[10]

The moral poverty of peoples

The welcome received by the *Catechism of the Catholic Church* in itself alone shows the need for 'reference points' which is felt by our contemporaries. Reflecting trends of opinion and fashion, the social communication media often convey complacent messages excusing everything and resulting in unbounded permissivism. The dignity and stability of the family thus get disregarded or distorted. And consequently, many young people come to think of almost everything as being objectively indifferent: the one point of reference being what is conducive to the well-being of the individual, and the end often justifying the means. Now, let us admit it, a society with no values becomes 'hostile' to human beings, who then become the victims of personal profit, the brutal exercise of authority, swindling and criminality. All too many people today are bitterly experiencing this, and I know that statesmen are aware of these grave problems, for they find themselves having to tackle them every day.

Sometimes one gets the impression of a will, on the part of some people, to relegate religion to the sphere of the private, on the pretext that believers' convictions and norms of behaviour would be synonymous with regression or an attack on freedom. The Catholic Church, present within every nation on earth, and the Holy See, a member of the international community, have no desire whatever to impose judgements or precepts, but only to offer the witness of their conception of humanity and history, knowing this to proceed from a divine Revelation. Society cannot disregard this original contribution without impoverishing itself and impairing the freedom of thought and expression of many, many of its citizens.

Though the Gospel of Jesus Christ does not have prefabricated answers to offer for the manifold social and economic problems afflicting mankind today, it does, however, show what is important in God's eyes and hence important for the destiny of mankind. And this is what Christians are offering to anyone who is willing to listen. Difficulties notwithstanding, the Catholic Church, for her part, will go on offering her own disinterested collaboration in helping people, as the century ends, to become more enlightened and to realize how to liberate themselves from the idols of the day. The sole ambition of Christians is to bear witness to the fact that they understand personal and collective history in terms of the meeting of God with human beings. And Christmas is the clearest manifestation of this.[11]

Guidelines for a just and constructive political system

Warsaw, Moscow, Budapest, Berlin, Prague, Bucharest – to mention only capitals – have practically speaking, been stages in a long pilgrimage to freedom. We owe homage to the peoples who, at the price of immense sacrifice, have bravely undertaken this pilgrimage, and also to the responsible politicians who have encouraged them. The most admirable thing in the events which we have witnessed is that whole peoples have spoken up: women, youngsters and men have overcome fear. The human person has displayed the inexhaustible resources of dignity, courage and freedom that it guards within. In countries where for years one party has dictated what truth is to be believed and what meaning is to be given to history, our brothers and sisters have shown that it is impossible to stifle the fundamental freedom which give a sense of direction to human life: freedom of thought, of conscience, of religion, of expression, of political and cultural pluralism.

These aspirations expressed by peoples must also be met by the constitutions of all European nations. Ideological neutrality, the dignity of the human person as the source of rights, the priority of the person as against society, respect for legal norms democratically accepted, pluralism in the way society is organized: all these are irreplaceable values, without which it is impossible to build a lasting home common to East and West, accessible to all and open to the world at large. There can be no society worthy of humanity without respect for transcendental and abiding values. When we make ourselves the exclusive measure of all things, without referring to him from whom all things come and to whom this world returns, we soon become slaves to our own finite state. The believer, however, knows from experience that we are only truly ourselves when we recognize that we come from God and consent to collaborate in the plan of salvation: 'to gather together into one the scattered children of God' (John 11:52)

Hoping to solve society's problems by resort to violence is purely and simply a suicidal illusion.

Unbelief and secularization pose challenges which ought to be taken up by all believers, for they are called to bear witness together to God's primacy in all things. For this reason, besides the religious freedom that the State should guarantee them, it is essential that there should be better understanding and better collaboration between religions.[12]

Religion and politics

The Christian laity must not, especially at this decisive moment in history, shirk their responsibilities. Rather, they must bravely bear witness to their trust in God, the Lord of history, and their love of country by means of a united and consistent presence and honest, disinterested service in the social and political field, being ever open to sincere collaboration with all the healthy forces in the nation.

Love for one's own nation and solidarity with all humanity do not conflict with a person's ties to the region and local community where he or she has been born, or with the duties he or she has to them. Solidarity indeed runs through all the communities in which we live: first the family, then local and regional communities, then the nation, then the continent, then the whole human race. Solidarity animates them, draws them together in accordance with the principle of subsidiary, which attributes to each its proper degree of autonomy.

'Without me you can do nothing' (John 15:5). The words of Jesus contain the most convincing invitation to prayer, and with it the strongest reason for trusting in the Saviour's presence in our midst. For this very presence is an inexhaustible fount of hope and courage in the confused and troubled situations in the histories of individuals and peoples alike.[13]

'Pay to Caesar what belongs to Caesar – and to God what belongs to God.' By his answer Jesus indicates a line of behaviour valid not only for the historical situation at that moment, but for our times too and for all ages. He affirms that the world of religion is distinct from that of politics, each having its own aims, and each, for its own part, with the power to bind people's consciences. Religion and politics ought to remain separate spheres. But the religious individual and the citizen are lodged in the same person, and each person ought to be aware of his or her social, economic and political responsibilities and be prompt to discharge them. This is important at all times, and perhaps more important now than ever.[14]

Although martyrdom represents the high point of the witness to moral truth, and one to which relatively few people are called, there is nonetheless a consistent witness which all Christians must daily be ready to make, even at the cost of suffering and grave sacrifice. Indeed, faced with the many hardships which fidelity to the moral order can demand even in the most ordinary circumstances, the Christian is called, with the grace of God invoked in prayer, to a sometimes heroic commitment. In this, he or she is sustained by the virtue of fortitude ...[15]

An appeal for a united and Christian Europe

From Santiago, I, Bishop of Rome and Pastor of the Universal Church, cry out in love to you, ancient Europe: Come to your senses. Be yourself. Rediscover your origins. Requicken your roots. Once again live those authentic values which made your history glorious and your presence beneficial in other continents. Recognize your own spiritual unity while maintaining absolute respect for other religions and for genuine human rights. Give to Caesar what belongs to Caesar and to God what belongs to God. Do not be so proud of your achievements as to forget their potentially negative consequences. Do not be depressed at your quantitative loss of greatness in the world or by the social and cultural crises passing over you. You can still be a beacon of civilization and a stimulus to progress for the world.

If Europe will once again open her gates to Christ and not be afraid of opening the boundaries of her states, her economic and political systems, and the vast fields of culture, civilization and development to his saving power, her future will not be dominated by uncertainty and fear, but will open up to a new season of life, both internal and external, and beneficial and decisive for the entire world, threatened though it be by the clouds of war and the possible hurricane of an atomic holocaust.[16]

I shall mention three fields in which it seems to me the united Europe of tomorrow, open towards the east of the continent, generous towards the southern hemisphere, might resume the role of beacon in world civilization:

• First of all, by reconciling humanity with the Creation, by caring for the preservation of the natural world, of its fauna and flora, of its air and rivers, of its subtle equilibrium, of its limited resources, of its beauty which hymns the glory of the Creator.

• Next, by reconciling people with one another, by accepting one another as Europeans of differing cultural traditions or currents of thought, by welcoming foreigners and refugees, by opening up to the spiritual riches of peoples of other continents.

• Lastly, by reconciling us with ourselves; yes, by working to rebuild an integral and complete vision of mankind and of the world, as against the cultures of suspicion and dehumanization: a vision in which science, technical ability and art do not debar but arouse faith in God.[17]

In this Europe, aspiring to be united, there are many worries. There are many threats and tensions, actual and potential, urging in the opposite direction to that willed by Christ. Can the Church succeed in making herself the promoter of true peace? Can she succeed in deserving the blessedness reserved for the 'peacemakers'? Will she be able to transmit that reconciliation with which God has reconciled the world to himself, in the inter-human and international dimensions? This is the key question for the future of Europe and the world; a fundamental question too for the mission of the Church.[18]

An appeal on behalf of Africa

To the eyes of the attentive observer, the whole of Africa is undergoing amazing transformations. Everywhere there are immense problems still to be tackled. A stormy history has left a legacy of underdevelopment and ethnic rivalries and conflicts. Endemic poverty has produced countless material and cultural wants. The forces favouring progress and development do not always coincide with the best interests of the populations, and in many cases the policies of the past have left a weight of enormous international debt. But the winds of change are blowing. Many people of the African continent now realize that African solutions must be found for African problems; that individuals, families and groups must be put into a position where they can contribute to their own development; and that society, as a result, must become more democratic, more respectful of legitimate differences, more stable in its legal system, reflecting universally recognized human rights. The winds of change demand the renewal of economic and political structures, so that these will truly respect human dignity and human rights.[19]

No, Africa can never consent to being colonized anew. Her nations are independent and must remain so. This does not mean that help from other members of the family of nations is not necessary and desirable. Far from it, help is needed more than ever now. But to do any real good, it must not reflect a relationship of subjection, but of interdependence.[20]

IX

PEACE

The conflicts that arise around us,
the privations, the hardships that afflict
and torment so many human beings
from one end of the earth to the other,
are a challenge to all those
who profess to be followers of Christ.

There is military peace, social peace and inner peace.
In every way we ought always to hope that there will
be military peace and social peace, and we ought to
work together and do our bit to make sure that they
last and thrive.

Unfortunately, however, we know that every
century and age gives rise to nationalisms, territorial
claims, men of power who gain a moral ascendency
over the masses, and injustices that in turn give rise
to revenge and vendetta. Eventually we come to
understand that the greatest wealth is inner peace
and the resolve to keep the peace with everyone.

It is important to take note that periods of peace

can also become periods of corruption, of moral poverty, of self-seeking ambition, of a solely earth-bound and worldly mentality. On the other hand, we know that war is the consequence of sin and is the cause of immense suffering and horrible cruelty. The Christian knows Jesus' words: 'Peace I bequeath to you, my own peace I give you; a peace which the world cannot give, this is my gift to you. Do not let your hearts be troubled or afraid' (John 14:27). And hence the Christian knows that only in Jesus Christ known, loved and obeyed can there be peace. If you want peace, prepare for Christ's grace!

Human history and the yearning for peace

Never before in the history of mankind has peace been so much talked about and so ardently desired as in our day. The growing interdependence of peoples and nations makes almost everyone subscribe – at least in principle – to the ideal of universal human brotherhood. Great international institutions debate humanity's peaceful coexistence. Public opinion is growing in consciousness of the absurdity of war as a means of resolving differences. Peace is more and more clearly seen as the only way to justice; peace is itself the work of justice. And yet, again and again, we can see how peace is undermined and destroyed.

Peace is the result of many converging attitudes and realities; it is the product of moral concerns and ethical principles based on and fortified by the Gospel message.[1]

As human beings we live simultaneously in the world of material values and that of spiritual values. For the actual human being who lives in hope, the needs, freedoms and relationships with other people never correspond to the one or the other sphere of values alone, but pertain to both spheres. One may of course consider the material and spiritual goods separately, but it is better to understand that in human beings as such they are inseparable, and furthermore to see every threat to human rights, whether in the material or spiritual sphere, as equally a danger to peace, since it always affects the integral person.

Critical analysis of our contemporary civilization shows that, above all over the last century, it has contributed as never before to the development of material well-being, but that it has also generated, in theory and more so in practice, a series of attitudes in which, to a greater or lesser degree sensitivity to the spiritual dimension of human existence has been diminished owing to certain premises according to which the meaning of human life has been subordinated to all sorts of material and economic conditioning – that is, to the demands of production, the market, consumption, the accumulation of wealth, or the bureaucratization intended to control the processes in question. And isn't this too the result of having subordinated the human being to a single conception and sphere of values?

What is the link between what we are considering and the cause of peace and war? Given that material goods, by their very nature, give rise to conditioning and divisions, the struggle to acquire them becomes inevitable in human history. By cultivating this one-sided subordination of the human to material benefits alone, we shall not be able to overcome this state of need. We may mitigate it, or avert it in the individual case, but we shall not manage to get rid of it systematically and radically unless we promote and more widely honour the 'other dimension of good things' for everybody and all societies to see: the dimension that doesn't divide people but makes them communicate, makes them partners and unites them.[2]

True peace, founded on truth and charity

Christ, being peace – *true* peace – what other legacy could he have left us, other than this same peace? We have heard his words, recorded on the Gospel page. During this Prayer Vigil may they re-echo more strongly in our hearts and evoke a more convinced, more generous response: 'Peace I bequeath to you, my own peace I give you' (John 14:27).

If we look around us at this gathering tonight in Assisi, what do we see? Has the Lord Jesus truly bequeathed us peace? How is it, then, that there is so much violence around us and that in some of the countries from which we have come warfare is actually raging? What have we done with the Lord's gift, with his precious legacy? May it not be that we have preferred the kind of 'peace that the world gives'? A peace that consists in the silence of the oppressed, in the helplessness of the conquered, in the humiliation of those – individuals and peoples – who see their rights trampled underfoot?

True peace, the peace bequeathed us by Jesus, is based on justice, and bears flowers of love and reconciliation. It is the fruit of the Holy Spirit 'whom the world can never accept' (John 14:17). Doesn't the Apostle himself teach that 'the fruit of the Spirit is love, joy, peace' (Galatians 5:22)? 'There is no peace for the wicked, says my God,' the prophet Isaiah reminds us (Isaiah 57:21).[3]

The world needs peace, concord, mutual understanding. To the Church and the human race of every age, the Divine Master has left his everlasting testament of love: 'Love one another as I have loved you!' A sense of great sadness invades the mind at the thought of God's infinite goodness on the one hand, and on the other hand, human indifference, hatred and wars that obscure Divine Providence's plan on earth. You, with your prayers and your testimony of goodness, can offer a daily contribution to the cause of pacifying hearts and establishing peace on earth.[4]

Peace and Christian faith

The true centres of world history and world salvation are not the industrious, active capitals of politics and economics, of money and earthly power. The authentic fulcrums of history must be sought in the silent places where people pray. Here the meeting of the earthly world and the otherworldly world, and the meeting of the pilgrim Church on earth with the eternal and victorious Church in heaven, take place in peculiarly pregnant circumstances. Here something happens that is more important, and more decisive for life and death, than what happens in great capital cities, where people are so confident that they can judge the pulse of the times and control the steering-gear of world history.

To give the world the peace which the human race craves, politicians' conferences are not enough; agreements are not enough, nor are the politics of *détente* pursued by human beings – however important and necessary these may be. The world, tormented by discord, has need above all of the *peace of Christ*. And this is more than mere political peace. Christ's peace can only be established where people are disposed to forsake sin. The deepest cause of every disagreement in the world is people's abandoning of God. They who do not live at peace with God can only with difficulty live at peace with their neighbour.

Leaving God out of account when wanting to consolidate values of coexistence and concord precludes one from any chance of success. Wanting to establish social tranquillity in some mechanical way, without first solving the problem of what the values are to be on which it is to be based, leads to failure. Talking about peace in merely earthly terms and taking no account of our relationship with our Creator, produces scant and frail results.[5]

The question of disarmament

As disciples of Christ we are called in a special way to be peacemakers: we are called to overcome injustices, to renounce the use of force, to be ready to understand and also to forgive one another. In this, everyone can make a decisive and entirely personal contribution to peace on earth. Pledge yourselves to the understanding of peoples at the international level, to a progressive elimination of weapons of mass destruction, and to the joint efforts of all peoples to achieve peace and justice in the world.

Examine in the practical terms of daily life whatever is presented to you as 'progress'. We must be especially vigilant, if we are effectively to defend our earth and our life on it for the future. Regarding the problem of the environment and protection from radiation, we are no longer talking just about human life today, but also about that of generations to come. We must recognize the need for limitation and the dangers of proliferation. We cannot allow ourselves to do everything we are in a position to do. Restraint, self-control, self-denial – these ancient precepts of the Church suddenly become topical and modern again; in fact, they are absolutely vital to assure the survival of the human race tomorrow.[6]

The ecological question

Whereas at one time the decisive factor of production was the land and later capital – understood as a total complex of the instruments of production – today the decisive factor is increasingly humanity itself, that is, our knowledge, especially our scientific knowledge, our capacity for interrelated and compact organization, as well as our ability to perceive and satisfy the needs of others.

In their desire to have and to enjoy rather than to be and to grow, people consume the resources of the earth and their own life in an excessive and disordered way. At the root of the senseless destruction of the natural environment lies an anthropological error, which unfortunately is widespread in our day. We, who have discovered our capacity to transform and, in a certain sense, to create the world, through our own work, forget that this is always based on God's prior and original gift of the things that are.[7]

Theology, philosophy and science agree in their vision of a harmonious universe – that is, of a true 'cosmos', endowed with its own integrity and its own internal, dynamic balance. This order must be respected: the human race is called to explore it, with prudent caution to discover it and then make use of it, while safeguarding its integrity.

On the other hand, the earth is essentially a common inheritance the fruit of which should be for the benefit of all. 'God destined the earth and all it contains for all men and all peoples,' the Second Vatican Council reaffirmed (*Gaudium et Spes* 69). This has direct implications for our problem. It is unjust for a privileged few to go on accumulating superfluous possessions by squandering available resources, while multitudes of people live in conditions of misery, at the lowest level of subsistence. And we must now learn from the tragic dimensions of ecological degradation, how seriously contrary to the order of creation – which has mutual interdependence written into it – individual and collective greed and selfishness are.

Today, society will find no solution to the ecological problem unless it seriously reconsiders its own life-style. In many parts of the world, it tends towards hedonism and consumerism, while remaining indifferent to the damaging effects that flow from this. As I have already observed, the gravity of the ecological situation reveals how deep the human moral crisis is. If a sense of the value of the person and of human life is lacking, there is indifference to others and to the earth. Sobriety, moderation, self-discipline and the spirit of sacrifice should shape our everyday life, so that all need not be constrained to put up with the negative consequences of the heedlessness of the few.

There is therefore the urgent need for us to be educated about ecological responsibility: responsibility towards ourselves, responsibility towards others, responsibility towards the environment. This education is not something that can be based on emotion or vague aspirations. Its goal can be neither ideological nor political, and its programme cannot rest on a rejection of the modern world or on the vague desire for a return to 'paradise lost'. True education about responsibility involves a genuine conversion in the way we think and behave.[8]

The material poverty of many peoples

The earth has never produced so much, nor had so many hungry people on it. The fruits of growth are still shared out unevenly. In addition to this there is the widening divide between North and South. As you know, I tried to call the attention of people of good will to this problem in my *Message for World Peace Day* (1 January), in which I wrote: 'Thus a covert but real threat to peace is *extreme poverty*. By eating away at human dignity, it constitutes a serious attack on the value of life and strikes the peaceful development of society to the heart' (n. 3).

Faced with mounting poverty, making the poor grow more numerous and ever poorer, faced with such marginalization as unemployment painfully affecting the rising generations, cultural deprivation, racism, break-up of the family, and illness, the political leadership should be the first to be arraigned. The world now possesses the technical and structural potentials for improving living conditions. Today more than yesterday, everyone should have a chance to enjoy a fair and worthy share in life's banquet. The sharing out of the goods of the earth, a just distribution of profits, a healthy resistance to excessive consumption and the safeguarding of the human environment: these are most urgent of the duties incumbent on the public authorities.

Associating the citizens with the planning of society, giving them confidence in those who govern them and in the nation to which they belong: these are the bases on which the harmonious life of human communities is founded. Very often such phenomena as street demonstrations or the climate of suspicion to which the media of social communication give voice, are nothing else than manifestations of dissatisfaction and powerlessness over basic necessities which are being disregarded: not seeing one's legitimate rights guaranteed, not feeling oneself considered as having a share in the political and social plan, not glimpsing any beginning of a solution to problems that have been going on for years. Basically, all the problems concerning justice have as their main cause the fact that the individual is not sufficiently respected, not taken into consideration, not loved for what he or she is. We must teach people and teach them again to look at one another, to listen to one another, to walk together. This, of course, postulates that we all have a minimum of human values in common, the recognition of which can motivate convergent choices.[9]

The culture of life and the culture of death

The twentieth century will be seen as a period of glaring attacks on life, an endless series of wars and a permanent massacre of innocent human lives. False prophets and false teachers have known the greatest success possible.

Abortion and euthanasia – really and truly the murder of a genuine human being – are demanded as rights and as solutions to problems: problems of the individual, problems of society. This is a true massacre of the innocents.

Drugs, alcohol abuse, pornography and sexual disorder, violence: these are some of the grave problems requiring a serious response from society as a while, in every country and at the international level. But these are personal tragedies too, which need to be tackled with practical, person-to-person acts of love and solidarity, due to a great renewing of our own personal responsibility before God, before others and before our own consciences. We are our brothers' and our sisters' keepers.

The culture of life means respect for the natural

world and protection of the work of God's creation. In particular, it means respect for human life from the first moment of conception until its natural end.

A culture of life means serving those who enjoy no privileges, the poor and oppressed, since justice and freedom are inseparable and only exist if they exist for all. The culture of life means thanking God every day for the gift of life, for our value and dignity as human beings, for the friendship he offers us as we perform the pilgrimage to our eternal destiny.[10]

Humanitarian interference in defence of victim peoples

The emergence of the individual is at the base of what is called 'humanitarian law'. Interests exist that transcend the State: they are the interests of the human person, his or her rights. Today, as yesterday, human beings and their needs are, alas, despite the more or less binding texts of international law, still threatened to such a degree that a new concept has arisen within these last few months: that of 'humanitarian interference'. This description is very eloquent of the precarious state of human beings and of the societies they have built up. I had a chance to express myself personally on this topic of humanitarian aid when I visited the Headquarters of the United Nations Organization for Food and Agriculture (FAO) on 15 December 1992. Once all the possibilities offered by diplomatic negotiations, the processes envisaged by international conventions and organizations, have been set in motion and, this notwithstanding, populations are on the point of succumbing to the blows of an unjust aggressor, states no longer have a 'right to indifference'. In fact, it seems they have a duty to disarm this aggressor, if all other measures have already failed. The principles of the sovereignty of states and of non-interference in their internal affairs – while retaining all their validity – cannot, however, be used as a screen behind which one may torture and assassinate. For this is what it is all about. Certainly, international lawyers will have to study this new fact a bit more, to define its implications. But, as the Holy See is pledged to remind the world in the international appeals in which it often takes part, the organization of societies only makes any sense if it has the human dimension as its central concern, in a world made by human beings and for human beings.[11]

The social order for peace

The social order has humanity as its fulcrum. The human being is a creature designed 'in the image of God', with an inalienable dignity. From the value of humanity flows the value of society, and not the other way round.

Such a statement, however, is not to be taken as meaning that the individual and society are in opposition to one another. Far from it, human beings are by structure relational beings. Though our first and fundamental relationship is with God, our relationship with our fellows is also essential and vital. Such objective interdependence is raised to the image of those sublime and ineffable relationships that, according to Christian Revelation, characterize the intimate life of the Triune God.

From this view of humanity bursts a just view of society. Centred on the human person's aptitude for forming relationships, it cannot be conceived of as a formless mass ultimately to be absorbed by the State, but is to be recognized as an articulated organism, 'which is realized in various intermediary groups, beginning with the family and including economic, social, political and cultural groups which stem from human nature itself and have their own autonomy, always with a view to the common good' (Centesimus Annus 13).[12]

How many wars have broken out and how much blood has been shed in the name of ideologies which have been thought out in theory but insufficiently humanized by live contact with human beings and their tragedies and real needs! Thought is the greatest of human treasures, but the greatest of dangers too. It must be cultivated with an attitude which I do not hesitate to qualify as 'religious': for the search for truth, even when it concerns the limited realities of the world and history, always points the way to 'something further', crossing the border of the transcendent, and is thus, as it were, the antechamber to the Mystery.

There can be no doubt that we are living at an epochal turning-point. Behind us we have bloody, indescribable tragedies, from which we have miraculously emerged without yet coming to rest in that peaceful world we all wish for. So we are living in a very delicate passage of European and world history, disturbed by absurd conflicts against a planetary background marked by a thousand contradictions. We are none of us able to foresee the future. But we know the world will be what we want it to be. To this common expression of responsibility, we Christians want to make the contribution of our sound hope, founded on the certainty that we are not alone, since 'God so loved the world that he gave his Only-begotten Son' (John 3:16). He is a Father-God and Friend who, despite his apparent silence, has become our travelling companion.[13]

The peace and rights of the human person

We cannot ignore the historical experience of evil and sin, which can only be explained by the revelation of our First Parents' fall and the subsequent happenings down the human generations. 'In the course of history,' says the Council, 'the use of temporal things has been tarnished by serious defects' (*Apostolicam actuositatem* 7). Today too, not a few, instead of mastering things in accordance with God's plan and ordinance, as progress in science and technology would permit, rely excessively on their new powers, becoming enslaved to them and deriving great harm from them as well.

The Church's task is to help people rightly to orientate the whole temporal order and direct it to God through Christ. The Church thus makes herself the servant of mankind, and 'the lay faithful participate in the mission of service to the person and society' (Christifideles laici 36).

In this connection one must above all take note that the laity are called to contribute to the promotion of the person, for this is particularly necessary and urgent today. It is a question of saving – and often of re-establishing – the central value of the human being who, precisely because of being a person, can never be 'treated as an object to be used, or as a means or as a thing' (Christifideles laici 37).

As for personal dignity, all men are equal one with another; no discrimination can be admitted, neither racial, sexual, social, cultural, political, nor geographical. With the differences arising from the circumstances of place and time in which each of us has been born, we owe the duty of showing solidarity by active human and Christian support, translated into practical forms of justice and charity, as St Paul explained and recommended to the Corinthians: 'It is not that you ought to relieve other people's needs and leave yourselves in hardship; but there should be a fair balance. Your surplus may fill their deficit, and another time their surplus may fill your deficit. So there may be a fair balance' (2 Corinthians 8:13–14).[14]

No more war!

Our Father! Father of men, Father of peoples. Father of all peoples living on earth. Father of the peoples of Europe. Of the peoples of the Balkans.

Father of the peoples belonging to the family of the South Slavs! Father of the peoples who here, in this peninsula, have written their history over the centuries. Father of the peoples touched, alas, not for the first time by the cataclysm of war.

Our Father ... I, Bishop of Rome, the first Slav Pope, kneel before you and cry: From plague, famine and war – deliver us! I know many will join me in this prayer. Not only in Sarajevo, in Bosnia and Herzegovina, but all over Europe and beyond its boundaries.

Forgive us our trespasses as we forgive those who trespass against us ... With these words we touch the crucial question. Christ himself told us about this when dying on the cross; he said, referring to his killers: 'Father, forgive them; they do not know what they are doing' (Luke 23:34).

The history of mankind, of peoples and of nations, is full of mutual grudges and injustices. What an important effect those historic words have had, addressed by the Polish Bishops to their German colleagues at the end of the Second Vatican Council: 'We forgive and ask forgiveness!' If peace has been possible in that particular region of Europe, this would seem to have come about precisely thanks to the attitude so effectively expressed in these words.

Today let us pray very hard that a similar gesture may again be made: 'We forgive and ask forgiveness' for our brothers in the Balkans! Without this attitude, peace is hard to build. The spiral of 'guilt' and 'punishment' will never cease unless at some point we can manage to forgive. Forgiving does not mean forgetting. If memory is the law of history, forgiveness is the power of God, the power of Christ, at work in the affairs of individuals and peoples.

'Father, forgive them!' (Luke 23:34). Christ offers forgiveness from his Cross and begs us too to follow him on the arduous way of the Cross to gain his peace. Only by accepting his invitation can we prevent selfishness, nationalism and violence from continuing to sow destruction and death.

Evil in each of its manifestations constitutes a mystery of iniquity, before which, clearly and decisively, rings out God's voice as we have heard in our first Reading today: 'Thus says the High and Exalted one ... I live in the holy heights but I am with the oppressed and humiliated' (Isaiah 57:15). For all, these prophetic words contain an invitation to serious examination of conscience.

God is on the side of the oppressed: he is beside the parents weeping for their murdered children, he hears the helpless crying of those who are trampled on and defenceless, he feels for women subjected to rape, he is near refugees being forced to leave their lands and homes. He does not forget the sufferings of widows, youngsters and children. They are his own people who are dying.

We must put an end to such barbarity! Enough of war! No more destructive rage! No longer can we tolerate a situation producing nothing but the fruits of death: killings, towns destroyed, economies wrecked, hospitals running out of drugs, the sick and aged abandoned, families in tears and torn apart. We must achieve a just peace as soon as possible. Peace *is* possible, once we all recognize the priority of moral values over the false claims of race or might.[15]

Peace is not Utopia

Peace, if we really want it, is always possible!

For it to be built on foundations of justice and truth, it must first of all be besought of God. It was for this that in January 1993 I invited Catholics and representatives of other Christian confessions and of non-Christian religions to Assisi, and promoted a similar service in St Peter's Basilica to conclude the Week of Prayer for Christian Unity.

Prayer must, however, be accompanied by the generous activity of people of good will. We must promote a culture of peace, inspired by feelings of tolerance and universal solidarity. A culture of this sort does not drive out healthy patriotism but keeps it remote from narrow, exacerbated nationalism. It can mould great and noble minds, well aware that the wounds produced by hatred are not cured by rancour but rather by the therapy of patience and the balm of forgiveness: forgiveness to be sought and granted with humble and generous magnanimity.

Without this culture of peace, war for ever lies in ambush, smouldering under the ashes of fragile treaties. In Christian hope, therefore, I want to take advantage of this solemn occasion to raise a heartfelt plea: give up the language of arms for good, and let all hearts be open to the thrilling task of building peace![16]

The present tragic divisions and tensions should not make us forget that there are many elements that unite peoples who today are at war, and it is urgent and only right that we should gather up everything that unites – and that is not little – with which to rebuild new vistas of brotherly solidarity.

In this time of suffering I must stress that peace in the Balkans will be no Utopia! It has to be seen in terms of historical realism. For centuries, the peoples of these regions have accepted one another, exchanging much over the years in the spheres of art, language, writing and popular culture. And is not that tradition of religious tolerance – never failing over a span of some one thousand years, even in the darkest periods – also a common heritage? No, it is quite wrong to blame the phenomenon of nationalistic intolerance which is now raging in these regions on religion! This is true not only for the Christians of various confessions, on whom God is calling to make an extraordinary commitment to regaining full communion, but also for the believers of other religions, especially the Moslems, who have consolidated an outstanding presence in the Balkans, within the framework of respectful and civilized coexistence.[17]

X

RELIGIONS

God desires the salvation of everyone.
In a mysterious but real way, he is present in all.
Humanity forms one single family,
since all human beings
have been created by God in his own image.
All have a common destiny,
since they are called to find fullness of life
in God.

Given the present state of society, where culture has increased and more and more peoples and life-styles are blending together, inter-confessional and inter-religious dialogue has become an absolute necessity: for, above all, today we need to know how to live with people who are different from us, in the religious field as much as in any other.

Inter-religious dialogue is not capitulation to error, not acceptance of religious syncretism, not good-natured, superficial tolerance. Dialogue respects consciences; dialogue recognizes the value of the various

religions; above all, dialogue is concerned with per-
sonal witness, so as to exert a spiritual influence and
arouse a yearning for the true, unique religion – the
one willed by God himself.

In this sense, we can no longer go back: Revealed
Truth remains with all its religious and moral content,
and commitment to the Truth remains the duty and
mission of the Church and every Catholic Christian.

As to the eternal salvation of those who do not
believe (sceptics, agnostics, atheists and people who
are actually against God) and of those who do
believe but not as we do, this must of course be
entirely entrusted to the justice and goodness of the
Most High.

Ecumenism: its interpretation and meaning

The Church sees herself as a sacrament, or sign and
instrument of our intimate union with God and of
the unity of the whole human race'. And so she sees
herself in relation to the entire and constantly growing human family. She sees herself in universal
dimensions. She sees herself on the ways of ecumenism – that is, of the unity of all Christians, for
which Christ himself prayed and which is of indis-
putable urgency in our own day. She also sees herself
in dialogue with the followers of non-Christian religions and with all people of good will. This sort of
dialogue is a dialogue of salvation, which should also
serve world peace and justice on earth.[1]

The divisions that still exist among us weaken the vitality of the Gospel and become a scandal for the world, especially when we seem to be preaching 'a Kingdom divided against itself' (Luke 11:17). The credibility of the Gospel is diminished by our divisions.

Christian unity should of course be prayed for as God's gift, and we trust in the fact that it will be guaranteed in accordance with the Lord's will. Christians should never stop praying and denying themselves for unity. They are called, furthermore, to sustain the efforts for theological dialogue, mutual witness and practical co-operation which have been put into effect by their respective communities.

Ecumenical co-operation, important as it is, must not become an end in itself, since this could obscure its real purpose, which is the quest for fully visible unity among separated Christians.[2]

One of the greatest truths of which we are the humble custodians is the doctrine of the unity of the Church, a unity obscured on the Church's human face by every form of sin, but which subsists in the Catholic Church indestructible (cf. *Lumen gentium* 8; *Unitatis redintegratio* 2–3). Consciousness of sin calls us constantly to conversion. Christ's will prompts us to work seriously and ceaselessly for unity with all our fellow Christians, being aware that the unity we seek is that of the perfect Faith, a unity in truth and love.

We must pray and study together, remembering, however, that inter-communion among divided Christians is not the answer to Christ's call for perfect unity. With God's help, we mean to go on humbly and resolutely working to remove the real divisions still existing, and thus to restore that full unity in the Faith, which is the condition for sharing in the Eucharist (cf. Allocution of 4 May 1979). The Ecumenical Council's charge applies to each one of us; so too the Testament of Paul VI, which says about ecumenism: 'Let the work of drawing closer to our separated brethren be pursued with much understanding, with much patience, with great love; but without deviating from true Catholic doctrine.'[3]

Inter-religious dialogue and prayer

Contacts with the religions of Asia, especially Hinduism and Buddhism, which are noted for their contemplative spirit, for their methods of meditation and for their asceticism, can greatly contribute to the inculturalization of the Gospel in that continent. A wise exchange between Catholics and the followers of other traditions can help to discern points of contact in spirituality and in the expression of religious beliefs, while not ignoring the differences. Such discernment is all the more pressing where people have lost the roots of their own traditions and are seeking other sources of spiritual support and enrichment. The growth of the so-called new or alternative religious movements is a sign of how widespread this tendency is.⁴

Throughout my pontificate, my constant concern has been to discharge this twofold mission of proclamation and dialogue. In the course of my pastoral visits all over the world, I have tried to encourage and confirm the faith of Catholics, and of other Christians too. At the same time I have been happy to meet the leaders of all religions in the hope of promoting greater inter-religious understanding and co-operation for the good of the human family.

To the Buddhist community, which reflects many traditions both Asiatic and American: I should respectfully like to show my esteem for your life-style based on compassion, on loving-kindness and on the desire for peace, prosperity and harmony for all living beings. May we all show similar compassion and loving-kindness in promoting the true well-being of humanity.

To the Islamic community: I share your belief that humanity owes its existence to the One and Merciful God who made heaven and earth. In a world where God is denied or disobeyed, in a world which is experiencing so much suffering and which is so much in need of divine mercy, together let us try to be brave bearers of hope.

To the Hindu community: I fully share your concern for inner peace and for world peace based not on purely mechanistic or materialistic political considerations but on purification of the self, on altruism, on love and understanding for all. May all the minds of all peoples be impregnated with this sort of love and understanding.

To the Jewish community: I confirm the conviction of the Second Vatican Council, according to which the Church 'cannot forget that she received the revelation of the Old Testament by way of the people with whom God in his inexpressible mercy established the Old Covenant. Nor can she forget that she draws nourishment from that good olive tree onto which the wild olive branches of the Gentiles have been grafted, (cf. Romans 11:17–24; *Nostra Aetate* 4). With you, I am opposed to every form of anti-semitism. Let us commit ourselves to hastening the day when all peoples and nations may live in safety, harmony and peace.[5]

God desires the salvation of everyone. In a mysterious but real way, he is present in all. Humanity forms one single family, since all human beings have been created by God in his own image. All have a common destiny, since they are called to find fullness of life in God. Among human beings, then, differences of creed notwithstanding, there is a mystery of unity, of which Christians are well aware.

So that the mystery of unity may be fully realized and that 'perfect harmony of thought and feeling' of which St Paul speaks may come about, Christians should enter into the dialogue of salvation with everyone: a dialogue which God has been offering to the world throughout the centuries and which, faithful to the divine initiative, the Church is actively pursuing.[6]

The Catholic Church is in favour of dialogue: dialogue with Christians of other churches and ecclesial communities, dialogue with believers in other spiritual families, and dialogue even with those who profess no religion at all. She wishes to establish positive, constructive relations with individuals and human groups of differing belief with a view to mutual enrichment.

All this has to be done freely. For the Gospels underline that Jesus never compelled anyone. To the Apostles, Christ said: 'If you wish, follow me'; to the sick: 'If you wish, you can be cured.' Each one has to respond freely and completely responsibly to God's appeal. The Church regards religious freedom as an inalienable right, a right which goes with the duty of seeking the truth. Only in a climate of respect for the freedom of the individual can inter-religious dialogue develop and bear fruit.

This dialogue is not concerned solely with past and present values. It looks to the future too. It involves collaboration for the purpose of 'together preserving and promoting peace, liberty, social justice and moral values for the benefit of all' (*Nostra Aetate* 3).[7]

Catholicism and the historic religions

Even though the Church willingly acknowledges how much of truth and holiness there is in the religious traditions of Buddhism, Hinduism and Islam – reflections of that Truth that gives light to everyone – this does not lessen her duty and determination unhesitatingly to proclaim Jesus Christ, who is 'the way, the truth and the life' (John 14:6; cf. *Nostra Aetate* 2). We must not forget the Magisterium of Pope Paul VI on this topic: 'Neither respect and esteem for these religions nor the complexity of the questions raised is an invitation to the Church to withhold from these non-Christians the proclamation of Jesus Christ' (*Evangelii nuntiandi* 53). The fact that followers of other religions can receive God's grace and be saved by Christ, independently of the ordinary means established by him, does not therefore negate the appeal to faith and baptism that God desires for all peoples (cf. *Ad Gentes* 7). It is a contradiction of the Gospel and of the authentic nature of the Church to assert, as some indeed do, that the Church is only one way of salvation among many, and that her mission regarding the followers of other religions should be no more than to help them follow those religions better.[8]

Judaism

The decisive turning-point in the Catholic Church's relations with Judaism and individual Jews was brought about by these brief but lapidary paragraphs in *Nostra Aetate* 4. We are all aware of their many riches but three points are especially relevant. I should like to emphasize them here, before you, on this truly unique occasion.

The first is that the Church of Christ discovers her 'ties' with Judaism 'by sounding the depths of her own mystery'. The Jewish religion is not 'extrinsic' to us, but in a certain way is 'intrinsic' to our religion. With it thus, we have a relationship that we have with no other religion. You are our dearest brothers and in a certain way, we may say, our elder brothers.

The second point brought out by the Council is that to the Jews as a people no atavistic or collective guilt can be imputed for 'what was done during the passion of Jesus' (*ibid., loc. cit.*) Not indiscriminately to the Jews at that time, nor to those who came after, nor to those today. And hence all pretended theological justification for discriminatory or, worse still, persecutory measures is groundless. The Lord will judge each of us 'according to our own deeds', Jews and Christians alike (cf. Romans 2:6).

The third point I want to underline in the Conciliar Declaration *Nostra Aetate* 4, is a consequence of the second: it is wrong to say, despite the Church's awareness of her own identity, that the Jews are 'rejected or accursed', as though this were taught by or could be deduced from Holy Scripture, either from the Old Testament or from the New. Further, the

Council had said before in this same passage of *Nostra Aetate*, but also in the Dogmatic Constitution *Lumen gentium* 6, quoting St Paul in his Letter to the Romans, that the Jews 'remain very dear to God' and that 'his call to them can never be revoked' (Romans 11:28f.).

It is no secret that the fundamental divergence from our common beginnings was our Christians' adherence to the person and teaching of Jesus of Nazareth, a son of your people, which also gave birth to the Virgin Mary, the Apostles, 'the pillars on which the Church stands', and most of the members of the early Christian community. But this adherence is set in the order of faith, that is, in the free assent of intellect and heart guided by the Spirit, and can never be the object of external pressure in one direction or the other; this is why we are willing to deepen our dialogue in sincerity and friendship, respecting one another's deeply held convictions and taking the elements of Revelation which we have in common, our 'great spiritual heritage' (*Nostra Aetate, loc. cit.*) as our basis.'

The Church's relations with Islam

I am convinced that the great traditions of Islam, such as hospitality to strangers, loyalty in friendship, patience in adversity, the importance given to faith in God, are so many principles which should allow us to overcome inadmissible sectarian attitudes. With all my heart I wish, if the Muslim faithful find – and rightly so – the essential requirements for meeting the demands of their religion in countries of Christian tradition today, that Christians will in their turn be able to benefit from comparable treatment in all the countries of Islamic tradition. Religious freedom cannot be limited to mere toleration. It is a civil and social reality having definite rights which allow believers and their communities fearlessly to bear witness to their faith in God and to practise all that this demands.[10]

The right to religious freedom in the civil sphere

Some principles contained in the Declaration *Dignitatis Humanae* of the Second Vatican Council:

> It is in accordance with their dignity that all men, because they are persons, that is, beings endowed with reason and free will and therefore bearing personal responsibility, are both impelled by their nature and bound by a moral obligation to seek the truth, especially religious truth. They are also bound to adhere to the truth once they come to know it and direct their whole lives in accordance with the demands of truth (*Dignitatis Humanae* 2).

> The practice of religion of its very nature consists primarily in those voluntary and free internal

acts by which a man directs himself to God. Acts of this kind cannot be commanded or forbidden by any merely human authority. But his own social nature requires that man give external expression to these internal acts of religion, that he communicate with others on religious matters and profess his religion in community (*Dignitatis Humanae* 3).

These words go to the heart of the problem. They also show how the very confrontation between the world's conception of religion and that agnostic or even atheistical attitude which is one of the 'signs of the times' of our own day, can maintain sincere and respectful human dimensions without violating the essential rights of conscience of any man or woman alive on earth.

The same respect for the dignity of the human person seems to require that when the just way of exercising religious freedom is being discussed or established in the context of national legislation or international conventions, institutions which of their nature serve religious life should be included too. By not allowing them to share this freedom, there is a risk of imposing norms or restrictions in a very intimate field of human life, and that would be contrary to our true religious needs.[11]

LIST OF SOURCES

I Faith

1. *Homily in the parish church of Santi Protomartiri*, Rome, 21 April 1985.
2. *Address*, Verona, 16 April 1988.
3. *Address to the Sanctuary of the Madonna delle Grazie*, Benevento 2 July 1990.
4. *Address to young people*, Paris, 1 June 1980.
5. *Address to scientists and students*, Cologne, 15 November 1980.
6. *To the Almo Collegio Capranica*, Rome, 21 January 1980.
7. *Address to the Pontifical Academy of Sciences*, Vatican City, 31 October 1992.
8. *Meeting with scientists at the Centro 'Ettore Majorana'*, Erice, 8 May 1993.
9. *Homily for young people*, Munich, 19 November 1980.
10. *To the Dutch Bishops on their visit 'ad limina Apostolorum'*, Vatican City, 11 January 1993.
11. *Meeting with the Laity*, Fulda, 18 November 1980.

12. *Address to members of the University*, Cracow, 8 June 1979.
13. *Homily*, Osnabrück, 16 November 1980.
14. *Address to Salesian Youth*, Rome, 5 May 1979.
15. *Address to young people*, Santiago de Compostela, 19 August 1989.
16. *Homily in the Indira Gandhi Stadium*, New Delhi, 1 February 1986.
17. *Address to the rural world*, Bahia Blanca, 7 April 1987.
18. *Homily*, New Delhi, 1 February 1986.
19. *Homily*, New Delhi, 2 February 1986.
20. *Dominum et vivificantem* 67, 57.
21. *Homily*, Viedma, Argentina, 6 April 1987.
22. *Homily* outside Munster Cathedral, 1 May 1987.

II The Church

1. *Homily*, Brisbane, Australia, 25 November 1986.
2. *To the Bishops of the Apostolic Region*, Provence Mediterranée, France, 22 December 1992.
3. *Address*, Troia, Apulia, 25 May 1987.
4. *General Audience*, 25 November 1992.
5. *General Audience*, 24 February 1993.
6. *General Audience*, 10 March 1993.
7. *Meeting with the Clergy, Religious and Seminarists*, Sarh, Chad, 31 January 1990.
8. *Letter to Priests*, Maundy Thursday, 1979.
9. *General Audience*, 10 November 1993.
10. *General Audience*, 24 November 1993.

11. *General Audience*, 1 December 1993.
12. *General Audience*, 26 January 1994.
13. *General Audience*, 22 June 1994.
14. *General Audience*, 13 July 1994.
15. *General Audience*, 27 July 1994.
16. *Address to the Catholic University*, Washington, USA, 7 October 1979.
17. *Address to scientists and students*, Cologne, 15 November 1980.
18. *Address to Professors of Theology*, Altaetting, 18 November 1980.
19. *Address to the Clergy*, Maynooth, Ireland, 1 October 1979.
20. *Catechesi tradendae* 57, 67, 68.
21. *Address to artists and journalists*, Munich, 19 November 1980.
22. *Centesimus Annus* 29, 51, 46, 32.
23. *Homily*, Miami, United States, 11 September 1987.
24. *Homily*, New Delhi, 2 February 1986.
25. *Homily*, Trivandrum, India, 2 February 1986.
26. *Visit to the 'Hogar de Cristo'*, Santiago, Chile, 3 April 1987.
27. *Address to cultural and business figures*, Lima, Peru, 15 May 1988.
28. *Address to leading politicians*, Buenos Aires, Argentina, 6 April 1987.
29. *Address to the Bishops*, Santiago, Chile, 2 April 1987.

30. *General Audience*, 3 June 1993.

III Prayer

1. *Audience for young people*, 14 March 1979.
2. *Address to the young*, New Orleans, USA, 12 September 1987.,
3. *Address to the young*, Benevento, 2 July 1990.
4. *Homily*, Viedma, Argentina, 6 April 1987.
5. *Homily*, Dublin, 29 September 1979.
6. *To the Milan and Alessandria pilgrimages*, 14 November 1981.
7. *Homily*, Strasbourg, 8 October 1988.
8. *General Audience*, 15 December 1993.
9. *Homily*, Uruguay, 7 May 1988.
10. *Homily*, St Peter's, 2 January 1993.
11. *Homily for the administration of Confirmation*, Turin, 2 September 1988.
12. *Homily*, Phoenix, USA, 14 September 1987.
13. *Redemptoris Mater* 52.
14. *General Audience*, 26 June 1994.
15. *General Audience*, 29 October 1978.
16. *Catechesi tradendae* 54.
17. *Homily*, La Serena, Chile, 5 April 1987.
18. *To the Basilian Poor Clares*, Albano, 14 August 1979.

IV Love

1. *Homily*, San Francisco, USA, 17 September 1987.

2. *Apostolic Letter to World Youth* for International Youth Year, 31 March 1985.
3. *Address to the young*, Foggia, 24 May 1987.
4. *Address to families*, Foggia, 24 May 1987.
5. *Address to the young*, Paris, 1 June 1980.
6. *Address to the young*, Belo Horizonte, Brazil, 1 July 1980.
7. *General Audience*, 2 April 1980.
8. *Angelus*, 26 June 1994.
9. *General Audience*, 5 May 1982.
10. *Homily*, Cologne, 15 November 1980.
11. *Apostolic Letter to World Youth*, op. cit.
12. *Angelus*, 10 July 1994.
13. *Homily at Mass on the 'Tres Cruces' Esplanade*, Montevideo, 1 April 1987.
14. *General Audience*, 10 August 1994.
15. *To the Bishops of the East Central Region of France on their 'ad limina' visit*, Rome, 28 March 1992.
16. *Homily for Holy Mass*, Perth, Australia, 30 November 1986.
17. *Homily*, Columbia, USA, 11 September 1987.
18. *Angelus*, 17 July 1994.
19. *Angelus*, 31 July 1994.
20. *General Audience*, 20 July 1994.
21. *Address at Willson Training Centre*, Hobart, Tasmania, 27 November 1986.
22. *Angelus*, 14 August 1994.
23. *To the US Bishops of the ecclesiastical provinces*

of Baltimore, Washington, Atlanta & Miami,
2 July 1993.
24. *Angelus*, 24 July 1994.
25. *Angelus*, 7 August 1994.
26. *Homily*, Foggia, 25 May 1987.
27. *Homily for Holy Mass*, Perth, Australia,
30 November 1986.
28. *Homily for the celebration of the Sacrament of Marriage*, St Peter's, Rome, 12 June 1994.

VI History

1. *Address to Italian Servicemen*, 1 March 1979.
2. *Catechesi tradendae* 29.
3. *Address at the Centro Italiano di Solidarietà*,
5 August 1979.
4. *Address to Religious Communities*, parish of St Pius V, Rome, 28 October 1979.
5. *Address to young people*, Buenos Aires, 11 April 1987.
6. *Dominum et vivificantem* 57.
7. *Apostolic Letter to World Youth for International Youth Year*, 31 March 1985.
8. *Address to young people*, Agrigento, 9 May 1993.
9. *Address to the sick*, Cordoba Cathedral, 8 April 1987.
10. *General Audience*, 27 April 1994.
11. *General Audience*, 15 June 1994.
12. *Homily for university students*, Vatican Basilica,
5 April 1979.

13. *General Audience*, 30 September 1987.
14. *General Audience*, 13 January 1982.
15. *Inauguration of Michelangelo's restored frescoes*, Sistine Chapel, 8 April 1994.

VI Evil

1. *General Audience*, 30 January 1980.
2. *Dominum et vivificantem* 37.
3. *Dominum et vivificantem* 46.
4. *General Audience*, 30 April 1980.
5. *General Audience*, 10 September 1980.
6. *General Audience*, 17 December 1980.
7. *General Audience*, 7 January 1981.
8. *Address to clergy and religious*, Santiago Cathedral, Chile, 1 April 1987.
9. *General Audience*, 14 January 1981.
10. *To the US Bishops of Alabama, Kentucky, Louisiana, Mississippi and Tennessee*, 5 May 1993.
11. *Homily for university students*, Vatican Basilica, 5 April 1979.

VII Work

1. *Address to workers*, Buenos Aires, 10 April 1987.
2. *Address to workers and miners*, Jasna Gora, 6 June 1979.
3. *Address to workers*, Turin, 13 April 1980.
4. *General Audience*, 20 April 1994.
5. *Address to Diplomatic Corps and Political*

Authorities, Asunciòn, Paraguay, 16 May 1988.

6. *Address to 'Builders of Society'*, Asunciòn, Paraguay, 17 May 1988.
7. *Sollicitudo Rei Socialis* 41.
8. *Sollicitudo Rei Socialis* 39–40.
9. *Homily*, Mazara del Vallo, 8 May 1993.
10. *Address to workers*, Sao Paolo, Brazil, 3 July 1990.
11. *Centesimus Annus* 42.
12. *Address to businessmen*, Verona, 17 April 1988.
13. *Address to management and work-force at the Istituto poligrafico della Zecca dello Stato* (National Mint), Rome, 19 March 1994.
14. *Address to workers*, Sao Paolo, Brazil, 3 July 1990.
15. *Homily to workers*, Magonza, 16 November 1980.

VIII The World

1. *Homily*, Cologne, 15 November 1980.
2. *Address to scientists and students*, Cologne, 15 November 1980.
3. *Address to the German Bishops*, Fulda, 17 November 1980.
4. *Address to seminarists*, Philadelphia, 3 October 1979.
5. *Address to university students*, Cracow, 8 June 1979.
6. *Homily*, Dublin, 29 September 1979.

7. *Meeting with the Public Authorities*, Bonn, 15 November 1982.
8. *Address to the 4th General Conference of the Latin American Episcopate*, 12 October 1992.
9. *Address to President Omar Hassan Ahmed el-Bashir*, 10 February 1993.
10. *Homily*, Khartoum, Sudan, 10 February 1993.
11. *Address to the Diplomatic Corps*, 16 January 1993.
12. *Address to the Diplomatic Corps*, 13 January 1990.
13. *Letter to the Italian Bishops*, 6 January 1994.
14. *General Audience*, 17 October 1993.
15. *Veritatis Splendor* 93.
16. *Act of faith in Europe*, Santiago de Compostela, 9 November 1982.
17. *Homily*, Strasbourg, 11 October 1988.
18. *Special Assembly for Europe, Synod of Bishops (conclusion)*, 14 December 1991.
19. *Address*, Khartoum Airport, Sudan, 10 February 1993.
20. *Address to the Diplomatic Corps*, Kampala, Uganda, 8 February 1993.

IX Peace

1. *Homily*, Drogheda, Ireland, 29 September 1979.
2. *Address to UNO*, 2 October 1979.
3. *Ecumenical prayer vigil*, Assisi, 9 January 1993.

4. *Meeting with handicapped children*, Assisi, 9 January 1993.
5. *Homily*, Kevelaer, Federal Germany, 2 May 1987.
6. *Homily*, Punta Arenas, Chile, 4 April 1987.
7. *Centesimus Annus* 32, 37.
8. *Message for World Peace Day*, 1990.
9. *Address to the Diplomatic Corps*, 16 January 1993.
10. *World Youth Day*, Denver, USA, 15 August 1993.
11. Address to the Diplomatic Corps, 16 January 1993.
12. *Centesimus Annus* 13.
13. *Homily*, Riga, Latvia, 9 September 1993.
14. *General Audience*, 13 April 1994.
15. *Homily*, Castel Gandolfo with TV link to Sarajevo, 8 September 1994.
16. *Address* at Zagreb International Airport, 10 September 1994.
17. *Homily*, Zagreb, 11 September 1994.

X Religions

1. *Apostolic Letter to World Youth* for International Youth Year, 31 March 1985.
2. *Ecumenical service in the Anglican Cathedral*, Kampala, Uganda, 7 February 1993.
3. *Address to the Bishops of the USA*, 5 October 1979.

4. *Address to the Plenary Assembly of the Pontifical Council for Inter-religious Dialogue*, 13 November 1992.
5. *Meeting with representatives of Historical Religions*, Los Angeles, 16 September 1987.
6. *Homily, Parakou, Benin*, 4 February 1993.
7. *Homily, Cotonou, Benin*, 4 February 1993.
8. *Letter to the Bishops taking part at the Bandung Assembly*, 23 June 1990.
9. *Address in the Synagogue*, Rome, 13 April 1968.
10. *Homily to the Diplomatic Corps*, 13 January 1990.
11. *Address to UNO*, 2 October 1979.

The Gospel of Life
A Message of Hope
Pope John Paul II
The Holy Father's New Letter to the World

In the wake of the massive worldwide sales for *Crossing the Threshold of Hope*, the Pope has written a stirring new letter offering, in his words, a 'message of hope'.

The letter goes to the heart of the most fundamental moral question there is: the value of human life. The Pope gives teaching on the various threats to life including social injustice, the arms trade, abortion, euthanasia and embryo experimentation.

'An inspiring exposition ... The ideals the Pope puts forward are ones which will always be difficult to realize, but in striving to do so we can be confident of building a better and more human world. What is clear beyond doubt is that we must make the unconditional respect for human life the foundation of a renewed society.'
Cardinal Basil Hume

Love and Responsibility
Pope John Paul II

Love and Responsibility is Karol Wojtyla's classic book on the subject of marriage and sexual morality.

First published in English soon after his election as Pope, it remains his most impressive book, and its thinking has underpinned much of his teaching since, particularly the 1993 encyclical *Splendor Veritatis*.

Based substantially upon the Pope's pastoral experience, the book is a profound examination of the nature of the whole human person which goes far beyond the scientific view. The most important concept discussed is that of love, and how a contemporary notion of sexual love can be changed back into the love of which the New Testament speaks.

'In the commonest view ... problems of sex are above all problems of the "body". Hence the tendency to allow physiology and medicine an almost exclusive right to speak on these matters – psychology is allotted only a secondary role ... This book puts the problem in a fundamentally different perspective. Sexual morality is within the domain of the person.'

The Word Made Flesh
The Meaning of the Christmas Season
Pope John Paul II

'Only by turning our thoughts to God at Christmas time can we understand the true value of each individual person without exception, beginning with ourselves. There is no other yardstick for human value, greatness and dignity. Therein lies the mystery of Christmas.'

The Word Made Flesh brings together a collection of addresses by Pope John Paul II, each focusing on a particular event in the Christmas calendar. With great warmth and wisdom, he reveals the glorious meaning of the mystery of the Incarnation, and explains how the foundations of ethical and social responsibility are contained within it. He urges us to translate the spirit of Christmas into our everyday lives.

Preached over a twenty-year period while he was still a cardinal in Krakow, the Pope's words reveal his unchanging belief in the importance of strong Christian values, the community and the united family. Both enlightening and thought-provoking, *The Word Made Flesh* delivers a message which will last long beyond the Christmas season.

Pope John Paul II
Michael Walsh

In the year 2000 there will be over 1,000 million Roman Catholics. Of these, two-thirds will live in the developing world, more than half in Latin America alone. For the 263rd pope, John Paul II, it is a momentous date. The Church that enters the new millennium will probably be led by him, and has been moulded by him in a dramatic fashion.

In this new biography, John Paul II is revealed as one of the most influential popes in the history of the Church. As the first Slav pontiff, he has looked East as well as West from Rome, and was a major force behind the revival of Eastern Europe and the overthrow of communism.

His faith is conservative, in common with his Polish compatriots. He has drawn more and more authority back to the papacy, turning back the tide since Vatican Two. In both respects he is in opposition to the more liberal style of the West, and particularly Latin America. So whilst his charisma and public profile have won him many proud supporters throughout the world, his style of leadership has divided the Church.

Michael Walsh's fascinating book seeks to examine the convictions of the Pope, and to find out how he came to hold them. It documents the dramatic events of his papacy through to the present day. It also asks the fundamental question: will he be able to mobilise the 1,000 million Roman Catholics behind his programme of change for the Church?